On Grief

On Grief

*Voices Through the Ages on
How to Manage Death and Loss*

Peter J. Conradi

Published in 2022 by Short Books
an imprint of Octopus Publishing Group Ltd
Carmelite House, 50 Victoria Embankment
London, EC4Y 0DZ
www.octopusbooks.co.uk
www.shortbooks.co.uk

An Hachette UK Company
www.hachette.co.uk

10 9 8 7 6 5 4 3 2 1

A CIP catalogue record for this book
is available from the British Library.

ISBN: 978-1-78072-480-5

Cover design by Luke Bird

Printed and bound in Great Britain by Clays Ltd, Elcograf S.p.A.

This FSC® label means that materials used for the
product have been responsibly sourced

In Memoriam: Robert Hutchison (1941-2017)
and Simon Edwards (1946-2020)

...Grief melts away
Like snow in May
As if there were no such cold thing.

Who would have thought my shrivel'd heart
Could have recovered greenness?...

from George Herbert, 'The Flower'

We read to know that we're not alone

C.S. Lewis in William Nicholson,
Shadowlands

CONTENTS

PREFACE

In late winter my much-loved sister Prue, younger brother Stephen and I made up a bedraggled and irritable convoy, with the shared intention of scattering our Mother's ashes in Golders Green crematorium gardens. Easy-going Stephen lugged the surprisingly heavy metal urn whose bottom – whenever the wrong lever was touched – kept opening prematurely, so that occasional traces of Mother spewed out onto our path behind us. It felt as strange and disrespectful to leave this trail behind us as it did to try to scoop it up by hand. We finally found the site dedicated to our father's ashes, and then proceeded to our stepfather's. Our aim was to divide Mother's remains equally between her first and second husbands, and Prue had brought a silver fork she had cavalierly collected from my kitchen to mash soil and ash together, a duty she now carried out. The fork did not suffer unduly.

A few weeks after this touching and comical interlude Stephen was diagnosed with a stage four cancer described in medical textbooks with the sinister adjective 'occult', meaning secretive. He died that August. Prue was diagnosed not long after. She died on 2 January 2013. If you include our young collie bitch, Sky, that made four rapid deaths in as many years. I was in my sixties and should not have been surprised. But I felt nonetheless unprepared.

How do you 'prepare' for bereavement? Christian faith once helped. So (perhaps) did the codes of dress and behaviour with which our Victorian ancestors ritualised and thus recognised different stages of mourning. Nothing much prepares us nowadays. Many theoretical books and articles about grief and mourning are published each year, but no 'theory' helps the bereaved much, precisely because grief so strips us naked and profoundly wounds us; and theory, like belief, can in such circumstances seem an insulting irrelevance. Nothing pre-cooked helps. No quick fix, no one-shot deal. No solution, and little comfort. Elizabeth Gilbert has pointed out that grief is a force of energy that cannot be controlled or predicted. 'Grief does not obey your plans, or your wishes. Grief will do whatever it wants to you, whenever it wants to. In that regard, Grief has a lot in common with Love.'*

About the possible violence entailed in grieving, a recent US radio programme was eloquent. *This American Life* chooses a weekly theme on which to hang different stories. In May 2021 they broadcast a programme wittily entitled 'Good Grief'. The first of its powerful narratives foregrounds Rob Delaney, an American comedian, actor, writer, and activist. Delaney in 2018 witnessed the death at

---

* *Eat, Pray, Love*, 2006. Among pre-cooked accounts, Freud's famous 1917 essay 'Mourning and Melancholia' might be included. This essay distinguishes the hard psychological work necessary for mourning, from melancholia, which Freud deems pathological, resembling depression.

home of his two-year-old-son Henry from a brain tumour; he records the experience of bereavement as ferocious and capricious.

Delaney couldn't believe that his baby had died, his experience of grief resembling psychosis. He forgot the PIN for his bank card and failed to recognise someone with whom he worked all the time. He felt physical pain, fatigue and confusion. And he punched himself in the nose and bloodied himself. 'I remember, I think the day my son died or the day after, I hit myself in the face. I don't know why I did it, but I gave myself a bloody nose.'

He had learned some skills from years of sobriety, which – when the intense storms of sadness and anger and confusion came up – helped him not to look away from the pain, try to manage them or push them away, 'but rather let them move through me as they needed to do... So I do try to be kind of brutal when I talk about it. And I feel like the worse of a picture I can paint, then the better friend I've been to you. It's going to be a real nightmare for a good long while. And you're going to cry, and you'll probably puke sometimes.' Delaney might well understand Olive Kitteridge's riposte, learning of a friend's recent bereavement: 'Then you're in hell."

For many of us, some resources nonetheless remain. One is the shared experiences of others. The testimony of survivors is available and helpful. 'We read to know that we're not alone,' as the character of C.S. Lewis says in *Shadowlands*, William Nicholson's play deriving from his book *A Grief Observed*. Writing can sometimes speak directly

---

* Elizabeth Strout, *Olive Kitteridge* (2008) p 318.

to us, be a comfort, a source of inspiration and strength; even, sometimes, of comedy. It is true that 'being well read doesn't help when someone who matters dies'.* However, if grief can feel like an obliteration of identity (about which more, later), reading can re-constitute some sense of community. And there is a bewildering abundance of possible material. Charles Causley's biting poem – not included here – 'Ten Types of Hospital Visitor' satirises the incompetent and aggravating onlookers who manifest either as vampires, know-alls, relentlessly cheerful or perhaps as needing the sick and the dying to reassure them. Unskilled in any case at simply sharing space. Both C. S. Lewis and Julian Barnes record their Causley-like anger at the ineptitude of survivors. They condemn those who attempt trite condolence; but at the same time they also censure those who avoid all or any uncomfortable mention of the dead. It seems that mourning and anger are related. Both are symptoms of powerlessness. No accident that the word 'grief' is related to 'grievance.'

The epitome of well-meaning inadequacy is surely Henry Scott-Holland's poem 'Death is Nothing At All' – often recited at funerals, with its saccharine cant about the dead person having simply gone into the next room. Scott-Holland, a priest at St Paul's Cathedral, read this poem as part of his sermon on the death of Edward VII in 1910. It ends: 'All is well./Nothing is hurt; nothing is lost./One brief moment and all will be as it was before./How we shall laugh at the trouble of parting when we meet again!' Perhaps this can comfort those of Christian faith. His poem

---

* Edmund de Waal, *Guardian* 21 May 2018.

may seem to others nonsensical, a consoling or insulting bromide.

A second resource is Buddhism in its earliest form. Here no false consolation is offered, no promise of future reunion in the Sweet By-and-By. When asked how the cosmos started, how it will end, and whether there is life-after-death, the Buddha preserved a noble silence and passed on. Buddhism has few if any outlandish or superstitious beliefs – no Virgin Birth, no Resurrection of the Body and no God either – to sign up to as entry requirements.* No affiliation is necessary, and there is nothing to join. Buddhism nonetheless characterises human life as having three non-negotiable Marks: Suffering, Impermanence and Egolessness (i.e. nothing lasts, because nothing has a fixed or permanent identity). And suffering in Buddhism is not something by which I am unfairly singled out or victimised, but impersonal and universal, defining life itself – not gloomily, just factually. The underlying thinking of this anthology is Buddhist. We are said to be the sole species that knows it must die; and yet we are also the species that finds death unimaginable and accordingly conjures myths to protect us and pretend death isn't real and that there might be 'bananas in heaven'.** Death and dying, it has been said, insult us.

Depression is one common reaction to apprehending the Three Marks; while the so-called 'Genuine Heart of Sadness' is its exact opposite. These two at first hearing sound so similar that 'feeling sad' and 'feeling depressed' are

---

* The Buddhist belief in reincarnation – arguably deriving from Hinduism where it supports and justifies the caste system – might be thought one bizarre entry requirement.
** See Yuval Harari's 2014 TED talk with that title.

phrases carelessly used as if interchangeable. But they are opposite states. Depression means repression. It entails closing off, shutting down, cocooning the bereaved from impermanence, loss and change. The 'Genuine Heart of Sadness', by contrast, is an open-hearted surrender to the contingency of life. From this point of view, grief is the background music of life itself.

If certain Buddhists have understood this polarisation, they are scarcely alone. Here Rabbi Nachman (1772-1810) comes to mind. This great 18th-century Hassidic Rabbi from Ukraine taught on the difference between broken-heartedness and depression and the difficulty of distinguishing one from the other. 'Having a broken heart and being depressed are two quite different things... Depression is rooted in the unholy "other side" and God hates it. But being broken-hearted and contrite over one's sins and shortcomings is very dear and precious to God... It would be very good to be broken-hearted all day. But this could easily throw most people into gloom and depression. You should therefore set aside some time each day for heartbreak. Seclude yourself with God for a given time and break your heart with regret .... Then be happy for the rest of the day.'

Perhaps William Blake evokes the Genuine Heart of Sadness in these well-known, beautiful and simple lines from the 'Auguries of Innocence':

Joy and woe are woven fine,
A clothing for the soul divine,
Under every grief and pine,
Runs a joy with silken twine.
It is right it should be so,

Peter J Conradi

We were made for joy and woe,
And when this we rightly know,
Through the world we safely go.

Olive Kitteridge first appears in the Pulitzer-prize-winning book of that name written by Elizabeth Strout in 2008. The book comprises 13 masterly, interconnected short stories, of which the last is 'River'. It is in this story that Olive meets the man who will be her second husband, Jack Kennison. She is bereaved, and so is he. She finds this out after watching him cry.

'My wife died in December,' he said.

Olive watched the river. 'Then you're in hell,' she said.

'Then I'm in hell.'

This exchange surprises Jack. Olive is a strange woman. A seventh-grade maths teacher, whose pharmacist husband died in a home, she has no brakes, no filter, and says what she thinks without minding how hurtful she might be. Blunt, erratic, bad-tempered, she has been called one of the great, difficult women of American literature. She's prone to 'stormy moods', as well as 'sudden, deep laughter', but she harbours a sense of compassion, even for strangers. She is one of those rare characters who seem to take on a life independent of the story framing them – like Falstaff.

Though Olive has trouble expressing love, she is gifted

with the ability to speak truth regardless of etiquette, comfort and context. In an earlier story ('Incoming Tide'), she climbs into the car of Kevin, an ex-pupil of hers whom she has not met for years, who is set on committing suicide, and somehow re-attaches him to life. Exactly how she achieves this is mysterious, but the reader notes that she is willing to share her understanding of the suicides both of her father, and of Kevin's mother. Communication happens at some deeper than conventional level.

Something similar happens with the exchange with Jack: through being willing to express the unsayable, she arouses his interest and before long he will find himself in an unexpected courtship with her. Olive Kitteridge's audacious acknowledgement of how deep the suffering entailed in grief can be, and how dark the journey is, is groundbreaking. Both for Jack and somehow also for the reader. And yet Olive Kitteridge is also an essentially comic character, one who – again, like Falstaff – has great resilience and keeps on surviving scrapes and conflicts. Survival and comedy belong together. And thus both comedy and survival have a proper place in any study of grief, that emotion experienced by survivors.

GILGAMESH: THE EARLIEST STORY OF GRIEF

Literature itself starts with a story about death and grief. *The Epic of Gilgamesh*, which originated four thousand years ago, features in its second half a King so terrified by death and by dying that he seeks to understand – then withstand and overcome – his own mortality.

Some 20,000 tablets in cuneiform script of this oldest surviving great literary text were discovered near Mosul around 1853 and sent to the British Museum, where they languished for sixteen years awaiting translation. Alarm and excitement followed: this story turned out to include a great flood and told of a man who builds an ark, and of a bird – exactly as in Genesis, a dove and a raven feature – released to search for dry land. The *Epic* was written long before the Bible: and such foreshadowings of the Biblical Flood were found sensational.

Over the past 150 years many more tablets in the ancient Akkadian and Sumerian languages have come to light, fashioned over two millennia. Scholars reckon that we still have only two-thirds of the whole so that, as with a living being, our understanding of the epic keeps changing. New tablets are still coming to light today.

Originally celebrating the glory of an epic hero and King, the epic was almost certainly recast around 1000 BC as a meditation upon the facts of life, and particularly on death.

Celebration gave way to lament. It starts with Gilgamesh, a heroic yet bad King of Uruk, abusing his power, a tyrant who exercises *droit de seigneur* on young brides and preoccupies the young with martial exercises, taking them away from their fathers so that his City can't function as it should and an outcry follows. He is superhuman, half-divine, and therefore has no counsellor or adviser to educate him. The poem criticises Gilgamesh, speaking truth to power.

In response the Mother Goddess creates a wild man from clay to match Gilgamesh and absorb his energies. Enkidu is hirsute, lives on all fours among herds of gazelle, visits their water-holes, eats grass with them and resembles an animal. In order to civilise him, a cultic Temple prostitute of high status is sent out to entrap and seduce Enkidu. Their coitus takes seven days and six nights, an act causing him to discover intelligence and wisdom, to be less of an animal and to connect with humans. He goes to the City, meets and challenges Gilgamesh to a duel, they fight, the result is a draw, after which they become intimate friends. They have supreme physical beauty and complement one another in their energy and aggression. Gilgamesh has found a mighty peer, a travelling companion, a fellow-adventurer. Deep love between them develops. Their adventures include killing a monstrous Guardian, fending off the advances of an amorous goddess and slaughtering the Bull of Heaven.

Through dreams Enkidu discovers that he is mortal and soon lies on his deathbed, weakening day by day. He cries more than once, 'My friend, fixed is my destiny, people go to their doom before their time.'

After he dies Gilgamesh weeps for him: 'My friend whom I loved so dear/who went with me thru every danger,.../the doom of mortals overcame him./Six days I wept for him and seven nights./I did not surrender his body for burial, until a maggot dropped from his nostril.' This horrifying image of fleshly corruption gets repeated.*

Enkidu's funeral is on the grandest conceivable scale. Gilgamesh summons his coppersmith, goldsmith and jeweller to make a funerary ornament. 'His eyebrows shall be made of lapis lazuli, chest of gold, body of… laid out on a magnificent bed…'** A whole forest of trees (boxwood, cedar, cypress) and a zoo of animals (bear, panther, cheetah, stag, jackal, lion, wild bull, deer, ibex) somehow get enlisted. The citizenry of Uruk are to mourn too. In one wonderful stanza, '[Gilgamesh] covered, like a bride, the face of his friend,/ like an eagle he circled around him./Like a lioness deprived of his cubs/he paced to and fro, this way and that./His curly hair he tore out in clumps/he ripped off his finery, like something taboo he cast it away./At the very first glimmer of brightening dawn,/Gilgamesh sent out a call to the land.'

Gilgamesh now begins his long final phase of wandering and quest. He roams 'through terrible mountains'. He crosses and re-crosses 'all the oceans'. His hair is matted, he kills and eats wild animals,*** he wears a pelt made from lion skin, he digs wells and spends his time – in a delightful phrase – 'chasing the winds'.

His grief for Enkidu begins to merge with terror at his own mortality. He knows he too is doomed to enter the Netherworld; he knows that – like his beloved friend – he

---

* Like so much ancient verse, the epic repeats ready-made formulaic phrases and whole stanzas. Repetition reinforces pathos.
** Tablet VIII E's funeral: pp 62 et seq.
*** Bear, hyena, lion, panther, cheetah, deer, ibex.

will lie there 'sleeping through the years'. This underworld has been figured in Tablet VII as a place of horrifying darkness and dust where souls languish in bird-form. 'Shall I be like him, and also lie down/never to rise again, through all eternity?' This open question gets repeated many times, un-answered.

So he sets out – in the path of the sun – to find Uta-napishti, the Noah-figure in the Babylonian Flood who survived the deluge and thus became the only human being to have been granted immortality. 'Of death and life he shall tell me the secret.'

His journeyings take him first to a boatman called Urshanabi and to a series of surreal ordeals: pragmatic lessons about his limitations, shamanic teachings about over-reaching. The Noah-figure compares the destiny of the King to that of the Fool: both experience the brevity and uncertainty of human life, and its futility.

Gilgamesh wants to know how Uta-napishti was granted immortality for surviving the Flood.* First of all he suggests Gilgamesh go without sleep for a week. He fails. If he cannot even overcome sleep, how can he master death, the 'big sleep'? Next, Uta-napishti tells him of a secret mystery of the gods: a plant granting eternal youth, which he is able to retrieve from the ocean by deep-sea diving. However, in one careless moment, he allows a snake to steal it. Realising that all his labours have been in vain, Gilgamesh weeps, tears coursing down his cheeks. ...

'What should I do and where should I go?/A thief has taken hold of my flesh/For there in my bed-chamber Death

---

* Tablet XI Immortality denied.

does abide/And wherever I turn, there too will be Death.'

The poem ends with an evocation of the mighty city of Uruk whose survival suggests perhaps that immortality belongs to the human endeavour itself, even though the individual perishes.

A tablet purchased in Baghdad in 1902, probably from Sippar on the Euphrates, provides a coda. Here a tavern-keeper advises Gilgamesh to enjoy life while he can and nurture the family that will bring him descendants: 'The life that you seek you will never find:/when the gods created mankind,/death they dispensed to mankind, life they kept for themselves.'

And Gilgamesh has of course gained literary immortality in any case.

Best remembered as the novelist who wrote *Sons and Lovers* and *Women in Love*, D.H. Lawrence was also a playwright and a notably accomplished poet. While his fiction can be laden with strange theorising, his verse memorably celebrates animals and also the minutiae of domestic existence with an admirable immediacy.

Be careful, then, and be gentle about death.
For it is hard to die,
it is difficult to go through the door,
even when it opens.

And the poor dead, when they have left
the walled and silvery city
of the now hopeless body
where are they to go, Oh where are they to go?

They linger in the shadow of the earth.
The earth's long conical shadow is full of souls
that cannot find the way across the sea of change.

Be kind, Oh be kind to your dead
and give them a little encouragement

and help them to build their little ship of death
for the soul has a long, long journey after death
to the sweet home of pure oblivion.
Each needs a little ship, a little ship
and the proper store of meal for the longest journey.
Oh, from out of your heart
provide your dead once more, equip them
like departing mariners, lovingly.

SIR WALTER SCOTT: STATUES OF SNOW

The novelist and poet Sir Walter Scott enjoyed 30 happy years with his wife Charlotte Carpenter. She bore him five children, among them Anne, who in 1826 greeted Scott on his return home to Abbottsford – as his journal records – with news of her mother's death. Scott, it seems, could not face watching her die: he preferred instead to fulfil his duties in court in Edinburgh. He had as a result subsequently to try to piece together her last days and hours, and his commentary on all this is the most moving section of his *Journal*.

Scott later wrote of marriage: 'Scarce one person out of twenty marries his first love, and scarce one out of twenty of the remainder has cause to rejoice at having done so. What we love in these early days is generally rather a fanciful creation of our own than a reality. We build statues of snow and weep when they melt.'

[Abbotsford,] May 16.—She died at nine in the morning, after being very ill for two days,—easy at last.

I arrived here late last night. Anne [his daughter] is worn out, and has had hysterics, which returned on my arrival. Her broken accents were like those of a child, the language, as well as the tones, broken, but in the most gentle voice of submission. 'Poor mamma

– never return again – 'gone for ever – a better place.' Then, when she came to herself, she spoke with sense, freedom, and strength of mind, till her weakness returned. It would have been inexpressibly moving to me as a stranger – what was it then to the father and the husband? For myself, I scarce know how I feel, sometimes as firm as the Bass Rock, sometimes as weak as the wave that breaks on it.

I am as alert at thinking and deciding as I ever was in my life. Yet, when I contrast what this place now is, with what it has been not long since, I think my heart will break. Lonely, aged, deprived of my family – all but poor Anne, an impoverished and embarrassed man, I am deprived of the sharer of my thoughts and counsels, who could always talk down my sense of the calamitous apprehensions which break the heart that must bear them alone. Even her foibles were of service to me, by giving me things to think of beyond my weary self-reflections.

I have seen her. The figure I beheld is, and is not, my Charlotte – my thirty years' companion. There is the same symmetry of form, though those limbs are rigid which were once so gracefully elastic – but that yellow masque, with pinched features, which seems to mock life rather than emulate it, can it be the face that was once so full of lively expression? I will not look on it again. Anne thinks her little changed, because the latest idea she had formed of her mother is as she appeared under circumstances of sickness and pain. Mine go back to a period of comparative health. If I write long in this way, I shall write down my resolution, which I should rather write up, if I could. I wonder how I shall do with the large portion of thoughts which were hers for thirty years. I suspect they will be hers yet for a long time at least. But I will not blaze cambric and crape in the public eye like a disconsolate widower, that most affected of all characters.

May 17. Last night Anne, after conversing with apparent ease, dropped suddenly down as she rose from the supper-table, and lay six or seven minutes as if dead. Clarkson, however, has no fear of these affections.

May 18. Another day, and a bright one to the external world, again opens on us; the air soft, and the flowers smiling, and the leaves glittering. They cannot refresh her to whom mild weather was a natural enjoyment. Cerements of lead and of wood already hold her; cold earth must have her soon. But it is not my Charlotte, it is not the bride of my youth, the mother of my children, that will be laid among the ruins of Dryburgh, which we have so often visited in gaiety and pastime. No, no. She is sentient and conscious of my emotions somewhere – somehow; where we cannot tell; how we cannot tell; yet would I not at this moment renounce the mysterious yet certain hope that I shall see her in a better world, for all that this world can give me. The necessity of this separation, – that necessity which rendered it even a relief, – that and patience must be my comfort. I do not experience those paroxysms of grief which others do on the same occasion. I can exert myself and speak even cheerfully with the poor girls. But alone, or if anything touches me – the choking sensation. I have been to her room: there was no voice in it – no stirring; the pressure of the coffin was visible on the bed, but it had been removed elsewhere; all was neat as she loved it, but all was calm – calm as death. I remembered the last sight of her; she raised herself in bed, and tried to turn her eyes after me, and said, with a sort of smile, 'You all have such melancholy faces.' They were the last words I ever heard her utter, and I hurried away, for she did not seem quite conscious of what she said. When I returned, immediately [before] departing, she was in a deep sleep. It is deeper now. This was but seven days since.

They are arranging the chamber of death; that which was long the apartment of connubial happiness, and of whose arrangements (better than in richer houses) she was so proud. They are treading fast and thick. For weeks you could have heard a foot-fall. Oh, my God!

We all wonder how we will face death – the moment when we recognise that our good fortune or life-force has run out or is just about to. Those lucky persons who die quickly might avoid such a reckoning; but few avoid a turning-point in life after which ill fortune and death beckon: recalling the moment Feste in *Twelfth Night* refers to when he says 'the whirligig of time brings in his revenges'.

In 1911, the Greek poet Constantine Cavafy (1863–1933) wrote a mysterious and wonderful poem about this, 'The God Abandons Antony'. It takes the form of a dramatic monologue and invokes the courage and dignity needed at such times of loss and defeat. He contrasts this with 'whining, the pleas of a coward'.

The odd title comes from the ancient Greek historian Plutarch, who records how, after suffering defeat at the hands of Octavian at the Battle of Actium (31 BCE), Antony and Cleopatra retreated to their power base of Alexandria, Egypt, where the two lovers had first met years earlier. One night, while besieged by Octavian's forces, Antony is woken by the sounds of instruments and revelry as if from a boisterous procession making its way through the city. He takes this as a sign that the god Bacchus, whom he regards as his personal protector, is now deserting him. The next day, Octavian's soldiers enter the city and Antony commits suicide, followed by Cleopatra.

This moment recurs, slightly changed, in Act IV Scene iii of Shakespeare's play, when four soldiers hear strange music, either in the air or under the earth, and ask, 'What should this mean?' The first soldier replies, ''Tis the god Hercules, whom Antony lov'd,/Now leaves him.' Shakespeare says Hercules; Plutarch says Bacchus. But it doesn't matter which deity abandons Antony: what counts is his gradual recognition of his destiny.

> When suddenly, at midnight, you hear
> an invisible procession going by
> with exquisite music, voices,
> don't mourn your luck that's failing now,
> work gone wrong, your plans
> all proving deceptive—don't mourn them uselessly.
> As one long prepared, and graced with courage,
> say goodbye to her, the Alexandria that is leaving.
> Above all, don't fool yourself, don't say
> it was a dream, your ears deceived you:
> don't degrade yourself with empty hopes like these.
> As one long prepared, and graced with courage,
> as is right for you who proved worthy of this kind
>   of city,
> go firmly to the window
> and listen with deep emotion, but not
> with the whining, the pleas of a coward;
> listen—your final delectation—to the voices,
> to the exquisite music of that strange procession,
> and say goodbye to her, to the Alexandria you are
> losing.

THE BUDDHA AND THE MUSTARD SEED

This Buddhist parable of the grieving mother describes a chronicle of devastating loss that today's refugees might recognise. The mother, here called Patacara, pregnant with her second child, is returning to her parents' home with her husband and small first-born. When a great storm blows up, she requests her husband to provide the family with shelter. As he is cutting grass and sticks, a snake bites him and he dies. Unsheltered, and wondering at her husband's long absence, Patacara gives birth and spends the night sheltering both children against wind and rain. The next morning she finds her husband dead and, distraught, decides to return home. A river – swollen from the floods – runs across her way. Unable to carry both children, she leaves her first-born on the near bank and wades through the raging current carrying her baby. Placing the baby on the far bank, she turns back to fetch her first-born. A hawk sees the baby, swoops and carries it off. Patacara raises her hands to chase it away, which her first-born takes as a signal to cross the raging current, sweeping him off to his death. Overwhelmed with grief, Patacara returns to her parents' home, where she discovers that it just burned down from a lightning strike in the storm. Her parents and brother are at that moment being cremated on a single pyre. At this point, she – rather understandably – goes mad and begins wandering around half-naked. Only on coming into the Buddha's presence does she start to recover her senses.

If the reader is inadvertently reminded of Gerard Hoffnung's Oxford Union bricklayer (each of whose disasters, by domino effect, triggers a painful successor), the intended message has of course to do simply with the ineluctability of suffering and impermanence. With her dead son on her hip, the stricken mother wanders from door to door, pleading for medicine to revive him. Neighbours ask mockingly, 'Where did you ever see medicine for one who is dead?' She is unconvinced. A certain wise man sees that her mind has been overthrown by grief, and although no one else will know of a medicine, tells her that 'the One of Ten Powers [the Buddha] will know'. He advises her to seek out 'the Greatest Person in the world who dwells in a nearby monastery... go into his presence and ask Him.'

The mother recognises that this man speaks truth. Carrying her son's body, she seeks out the Buddha, and supplicates him to 'please give her medicine for her son'. The Buddha proceeds to console her with art and simple cunning. 'Wander through the whole town starting from one end to the other,' he tells her. 'Wherever you find a home where there has never been a death, bring me a mustard seed.'

'Very well, reverend Sir,' she agrees, re-entering the town hopefully. At each house she begs for a mustard seed as medicine for her son. This they freely offer her. 'Before I'm allowed to take the mustard seed, I must ask you whether in this home has there not been a death?' In every household she learns that a father or mother, slave or child has died. Or they ask, 'Who is able to count those who have died here?' 'Then that is enough, I will not take it, the One of Ten

Powers told me I have to take it for him from a home where there has never been a death.'

After the third house she starts to realise, 'The whole city will be this way, this must have been foreseen by the Awakened One, who is beneficent and compassionate.' She becomes anxious, leaves the village and goes to the charnel grounds, and taking her son with her addresses him: 'Son, I thought there was death only for you, but it is not only for you, for the whole population it is the same, this is the Dhamma' (or Dharma in Sanskrit). She leaves her son in the charnel grounds, saying, 'Not a village Teaching, nor a town Teaching, nor is this a Teaching for one family alone, for the whole of the world… there is this Teaching of impermanence.'

Having spoken thus, she returns to the Buddha, who asks, 'Kisa Gotamī, did you get the mustard seed?' 'The business with a mustard seed is finished, reverend Sir, but give me something else for support.' The Buddha quotes her a verse from scripture (the Dhammapada) to the effect that even 'a clinging mind, intoxicated by children and cattle' – i.e. by attachment to possessions – will be carried away by death 'as a sleeping village is demolished by a great flood.' He teaches her the Dhamma which she now – wiser than when she left – is ready to hear and able to comprehend. At the end of the verse, as she stands there, she 'enters the stream' – in Buddhist idiom – and is soon established in the first stage of Awakening. She circumambulates the Buddha three times, showing him due reverence; then she goes to the local convent where she is ordained, and soon, after wise reflection, develops the insight to become an Arhat or saint.

A MOTHER'S LOSS: ALICE THOMAS ELLIS

Josh Haycraft, 17-year-old son to Alice Thomas Ellis, fell off a railway bridge and – after some months in hospital – died. She wrote this perfect quatrain, which recalls a 17th-century lyric, in his memory, and used it in 1977 as an epigraph for her first novel, *The Sin-Eater*. Before his accident she had discovered a dedication 'To Josh' that he had written onto the front page of the manuscript.

> All his beauty, wit and grace
> Lie forever in one place,
> He who sang and sprang and moved
> Now, in death, is only loved.

The idea that human life is grief-filled is scarcely a new one. The Latin words *sunt lacrimae rerum* – sometimes found on war memorials – come from Virgil's *Aeneid* Book 1 where Aeneas gazes at a mural in a Carthage temple. He recognises battles wherein his friends and countrymen fought and died during the Trojan War. Moved to tears, Aeneas remarks, '*sunt lacrimae rerum et mentem mortalia tangunt*'. 'There are tears for [or 'of'] things and mortal things touch the mind.'

These lines are variously translated. The poet Seamus Heaney rendered the first three words, 'There are tears at the heart of things'; while in his television series *Civilisation* Kenneth Clark offered, 'These men know the pathos of life, and mortal things touch their hearts.' The American poet Robert Fitzgerald (1910–85) gives us: 'They weep here/For how the world goes, and our life that passes/Touches their hearts.' These translations share a certainty about the tragic dimension of human life and death. All agree that this dimension needs to be grasped or negotiated.

The famous utterance has its own context. Aeneas recognises his own story and that of his peers; and this act of recognition brings him some solace that conditions both his grief and ours alike. He comes to see that he is among people who have compassion and an understanding of human sorrow; and this act of recognition of a common humanity in and of itself brings respite.

Wilfred Owen's magnificent sonnet 'Futility' encapsulates his sense of pity, horror and impotent outrage at a young soldier's death in the trenches.

> Move him into the sun—
> Gently its touch awoke him once,
> At home, whispering of fields unsown.
> Always it woke him, even in France,
> Until this morning and this snow.
> If anything might rouse him now
> The kind old sun will know.
>
> Think how it wakes the seeds—
> Woke once the clays of a cold star.
> Are limbs, so dear-achieved, are sides
> Full-nerved, still warm, too hard to stir?
> Was it for this the clay grew tall?
> —O what made fatuous sunbeams toil
> To break earth's sleep at all?

JULIAN BARNES: THE DEFEAT OF DEATH BY STYLE

In September 2008 the literary agent Pat Kavanagh was diagnosed with inoperable brain cancer. Thirty-seven days later she died. Her husband, the novelist Julian Barnes, writes about this loss in the final part of *Levels of Life* (2013). She is never named and he attempts no portrait of her. But he is too good a writer not to be interested in what is happening to him, and investigate it. He misses her body, her spirit, her 'radiant curiosity about life...' There are many moving pages of lamentation. 'Never see, hear, touch, embrace, listen to, laugh with; never again wait for her footstep, smile at the sound of an opening door, fit her body into mine, mine into hers.' He mulls over every detail of her decline, her time in hospital, return home, dying and burial. 'The last book she read, the last play they went to together, the last wine she drank, the last clothes she bought... the last this, the last that... her last complete sentence. Her last spoken word.'

Barnes compares bereavement with undergoing life-threatening physical violence; and he notes how anger and grief can segue the one into the other, grief into grievance. Both, after all, are symptoms of powerlessness. Some are angry at the person who has died for abandoning them; his own fury may be visited on friends, for their inability to do or say the right things. He also experiences resentment when others shy away from the facts, even the simple use of a name. He feels sharply the loss of shared vocabulary, of 'tropes, teases, short cuts, in-jokes, sillinesses, faux rebukes, amatory footnotes'.

Barnes is a knowing writer, hostile to the commonplace. But he is also self-knowing and he worries that he himself may appear 'less interesting' without his wife, and therefore more pedestrian. This is surely a remarkable perception, which connects with others. 'We are bad at dealing with death, that banal, unique thing,' he comments. He soon describes grief too, as 'banal and unique'. Perhaps he is better defended against banality than against loss? A small bridge in Venice where he and she wandered, is also described as 'banal'; his first novel, *Metroland*, satirised the banality of suburban living. His fine memoir, *Nothing To Be Frightened Of*, records his comic rage at the banal idea that he (and his work) might one day be forgotten, and he offers us stylishness as a defence against banality. It may be relevant here that both his parents were teachers of French, that he wrote the prize-winning *Flaubert's Parrot* and that he has been elected Commander of *L'Ordre des Arts et des Lettres*. His attempt to outmaneouvre oblivion with style and cool egoism belong in a heroic French tradition of thinking about the world. It recalls existentialism. His commitment to style at all costs helps lend *Levels of Life* some of its special potency.

He notes his impulse to report news to his wife in order to make it feel real to him, how constantly he talks to her, keeping alive their lost private language. He relishes hearing 'even the slightest new thing about her, a previously unreported memory, a piece of advice she gave years ago,

a flash-back of her in ordinary animation...' Even her appearances in others' dreams fascinate him, as if in this way
he can safeguard her communication with him and keep it
alive. Yet he also sees how changeable and how individual
'grief-work' is. Is grief a state, while mourning is a process?
They must overlap. He enquires what 'success' might consist
of, in mourning: does it lie in remembering? Or in forgetting? Some terrors die down. The temptation of suicide re-
cedes, cheerfulness and pleasure return. He finally comes to
see how grief is the negative image of love and its inevitable
dark reflection.

ELIZABETH BISHOP: 'ONE ART'

A poem by Elizabeth Bishop (1911–79) called 'The Bight' ends with the lines: 'All the untidy activity continues,/awful but cheerful.'

'Awful but cheerful' might stand as stock-in-trade for much of her poetic work, which negotiates the chaos of the world with brave reticence. And this is also how she appears to approach the pain of loss in her famous poem 'One Art': by levelling out everything that we lose, from door keys to people.

However, 'One Art' has hidden depth and power. As Meghan O'Rourke has explained, although the poem has multiple sources, it was at least partly triggered by the suicide of Bishop's long-time lover, Lota de Macedo Soares, whom Bishop had met during a brief trip to Brazil. The relationship evolved into a 15-year stay that Bishop later called the happiest time in her life. A landscape designer and architect, Lota killed herself while staying with Bishop in New York. 'Lota's family blamed Bishop for the death, and in many ways Bishop never recovered from it.'

The poem's gradually worsening catalogue of lost things ends by hinting at a terrible truth: that the loss of a beloved is a disaster. Bishop writes into the poem her own struggle to say what is – to her – unsayable, expressed in the stutter of that comparative word 'like': 'though it may look like

(*Write* it!) like disaster'. Drafts show that Bishop worked on this poem for several months and only when she came up with that little moment of self-consciousness did she consider the poem finished.

One Art

The art of losing isn't hard to master;
so many things seem filled with the intent
to be lost that their loss is no disaster.

Lose something every day. Accept the fluster
of lost door keys, the hour badly spent.
The art of losing isn't hard to master.

Then practice losing farther, losing faster:
places, and names, and where it was you meant
to travel. None of these will bring disaster.

I lost my mother's watch. And look! my last, or
next-to-last, of three loved houses went.
The art of losing isn't hard to master.

I lost two cities, lovely ones. And, vaster,
some realms I owned, two rivers, a continent.
I miss them, but it wasn't a disaster.

—Even losing you (the joking voice, a gesture
I love) I shan't have lied. It's evident
the art of losing's not too hard to master
though it may look like (*Write* it!) like disaster.

'DEATH IS NO MORE': LEO TOLSTOY

Not long after finishing his masterpiece, *Anna Karenina*, Tolstoy, now in his fifties, suffered the excruciating crisis that resulted in his writing *A Confession*. This treatise saw life as pointless while discussing four possible solutions: ignorance, pleasure-seeking, suicide or simple-minded faith. Before *Anna Karenina* Tolstoy had been the admired great writer who – it is said – saw human life on the analogy of a ballroom; afterwards, the revered sage increasingly rejected his own fiction and pictured life as a slaughterhouse.

Tolstoy now turned into the pacifist and Christian anarchist whose ideas of non-violent resistance influenced Gandhi among others. He became increasingly cranky and propagandistic; and his short novella *The Death of Ivan Ilyich* (1886) belongs to this new evangelising persona. It has been called the most powerful story ever written about a life approaching its end; the *Guardian* recently celebrated it as 'a hard, pitiless stare into the abyss, not just of death, but of human nature'.

Written in 12 parts, it begins with news of the death of a 45-year-old judge called Ivan Ilyich, after screaming in pain continuously for three days. Tolstoy shows us the commonplace, self-serving reactions of friends, vexed at having to travel to work up public shows of grief, or delay an evening's card-playing, while also mindful of the various new opportunities for career advancement Ilyich's death opens up.

The tale then goes back in time to the moment Ilyich sickened after falling from a ladder. He had been showing a workman how he wanted new curtains draped. Tolstoy evidently thinks he should have been thinking of his soul, not his redecorations, and arranges his punishment accordingly. Ilyich is shown throughout as a typical member of his class, a mediocre man suffering from what would later be called 'bad faith', not built to bear too much reality and hiding the savage truth of mortality under what the story calls enslavement to 'decorum': the world of bourgeois appearances or conventional good manners. Much of the power of the story comes from how recognisably Ivan Ilyich resembles each one of us.

His decline is described with a cruel forensic accuracy. His life is soon poisoned by his illness, which in its turn poisons the lives of others. His marriage – like Tolstoy's own – is unhappy and he experiences hatred of his wife, whose smart attire offends him. The reactions of others give him a gauge of how his illness is progressing. He starts to register the shock outsiders feel in seeing how his illness is changing his appearance. He notices a loathsome smell that comes even from his breath. Anger stifles him. And he is agonisingly, insufferably miserable. 'It cannot be that men have always been doomed to this awful horror' ... 'Can it be that [death] is the only truth?' ... 'Thrust into a dark sack... [he] cries at his own helplessness, at his awful loneliness, at the cruelty of other people and of God – and at the absence of God.'

Tolstoy offers Ilyich sources of consolation. There is his valet Gerasim, the healthy, handsome peasant whose ministrations, performed out of natural goodness, not pity, bring Ilyich some relief from his sufferings, both bodily and mental. Then there is Ilyich's gradual realisation that he hasn't lived as he ought. Though his mental sufferings are depicted as even worse than physical ones, he comes to understand that his official work... 'might not be the right thing... a horrible, vast deception covered both life and death...' Near the end he sees that he still has time to put things to rights. He experiences compassion for his wife and for his son. And finally what was torturing him suddenly drops away: 'In the place of death there was light'. 'What joy,' he exclaims aloud. His family witness another two hours of agony, but Ilyich himself – or so Tolstoy assures us – is at peace and dies at peace. 'Death is over,' he thinks to himself in his last moments. 'It is no more.'

Leo Tolstoy himself died, at a remote village railway station, aged 82. He had left his family home ten days earlier, in the middle of the night, walking out on his long-suffering wife of 48 years, to begin a new life in imitation of a peasant. 'I am doing what old men of my age usually do: leaving worldly life to spend the last days of my life in solitude and quiet,' he wrote in a cold letter he left for her.

He was taken ill on board a train and forced to get out at Astapovo, where the stationmaster gave him use of his house. His dying became one of the first international media 'events', attracting hundreds of his admirers and reporters from all over the world, including a Pathé News camera team eager to catch the great man's final moments on film (as well as some government spies). 'Tolstoy Is Better... The Count Is Very Weak, but the Doctors Say There Is No Immediate Danger,' blazed a headline in the *New York Times* two days before his death, when he was already drifting in and out of consciousness. He died of pneumonia on 7 November 1910.

ELEGY TO A WIFE: HENRY KING

This elegy is by Henry King (1592–1669). He was Bishop of Chichester, and married Anne Berkeley, in 1617. She bore him six children, although only two of these survived infancy. She died in 1624 and his most famous piece of work is his elegy for her, which breaks through its own artifice to communicate his grief at her passing.

Exequy

… Meantime thou hast her, earth: much good
May my harm do thee! Since it stood
With Heaven's will I might not call
Her longer mine, I give thee all
My short-lived right and interest
In her whom living I loved best.
Be kind to her, and prithee look
Thou write into thy Doomsday book
Each parcel of this rarity
Which in thy casket shrined doth lie,
As thou wilt answer Him that lent—
Not gave—thee my dear monument.
So close the ground, and 'bout her shade
Black curtains draw: my bride is laid.
  Sleep on, my Love, in thy cold bed

Never to be disquieted!
My last good-night! Thou wilt not wake
Till I thy fate shall overtake:
Till age, or grief, or sickness must
Marry my body to that dust
It so much loves; and fill the room
My heart keeps empty in thy tomb.
Stay for me there: I will not fail
To meet thee in that hollow vale.
And think not much of my delay:
I am already on the way,
And follow thee with all the speed
Desire can make, or sorrows breed.
Each minute is a short degree
And every hour a step towards thee....
  'Tis true—with shame and grief I yield—
Thou, like the van, first took'st the field;
And gotten hast the victory
In thus adventuring to die
Before me, whose more years might crave
A just precedence in the grave.
But hark! my pulse, like a soft drum,
Beats my approach, tells thee I come;
And slow howe'er my marches be
I shall at last sit down by thee.
  The thought of this bids me go on
And wait my dissolution
With hope and comfort. Dear—forgive
The crime—I am content to live
Divided, with but half a heart,
Till we shall meet and never part.

A STOIC DEATH: SENECA

> 'Why weep for the end of life? – the whole of it
> deserves our tears…'
>> *From Seneca's letter of consolation to Marcia*

A stoic outlook maintains that although we cannot control what happens to us, we can nonetheless choose what to make of it: so that, even in the face of terrible events equanimity might be cultivated. Stoicism has been called 'Buddhism with attitude', and might be boiled down to a series of precepts: live each day carefully and attentively.* Accept what cannot be changed. Remember that we are dust. Cultivate inner peace, calm and virtue. Check intense passions such as anger and grief by reason, will and courage: resist the urge to indulge grief with 'morbid delight'. Practise self-restraint in grief instead. Imagine the worst in order to train for the inevitable losses of life, and the better to appreciate people and things we love, who may not be here forever.

This leading philosophy of the ancient world has recently come back into fashion. Participants in the annual so-called 'Stoic Week', which attracts 20,000, are promised that Stoic life guidance can reduce negative emotions and

---

* See Brigid Delaney, *Guardian* 17 March 2020: 'How not to panic during the coronavirus pandemic: welcome hard times like a Stoic'.

improve overall life satisfaction. It has been mooted as an appropriate and helpful teaching during lockdown.

One of the leading Stoic philosophers was Seneca. Born in Cordoba in 4 BC, he was a statesman, brilliant orator and tragic dramatist (*Medea*, *Thyestes*, *Phaedrus*, etc.), and was as famous for his views on grief, on death and on dying, as for the manner of his suicide.

He served under successive emperors, many capricious. Proximity to imperial power could be dangerous. One story suggests that Caligula was so offended by Seneca's oratorical success in the Senate that he ordered him to commit suicide: Seneca survived only because he was seriously ill and Caligula was informed that he would soon die anyway. Then, in AD 41, Seneca was exiled under emperor Claudius for an alleged affair with the emperor's sister, of which he was probably innocent. The Senate once more pronounced a death sentence, which Claudius commuted to exile, and Seneca spent the next eight years on Corsica. His earliest surviving works date from this period.

In his 'Consolation to Helvia', his mother, Seneca comforts her in her various losses. Helvia's own mother had died while giving birth to her, and she had outlived her husband, uncle, and three grandchildren. Twenty days after one grandchild – Seneca's own son – died in her arms, Helvia received news of Seneca's Corsican exile. This final misfortune, Seneca suggests, prompted him to write to her. He advocated courage; he also advocated a strategy for inoculating oneself against misfortune by a process of rehearsal.

Dearest mother...

... I realised that your grief should not be intruded upon while it was fresh and agonising, in case the consolations themselves should rouse and inflame it: for in illness too nothing is more harmful than premature treatment. So I was waiting until your grief of itself should lose its force and, being softened by time to endure remedies, it would allow itself to be touched and handled... [Now] I shall offer to the mind all its sorrows, all its mourning garments: this will not be a gentle prescription for healing, but cautery and the knife... Let those people go on weeping and wailing whose self-indulgent minds have been weakened by long prosperity, let them collapse at the threat of the most trivial injuries; but let those who have spent all their years suffering disasters endure the worst afflictions with a brave and resolute staunchness.

Seneca returned to Rome in 49 AD, having been head-hunted by Claudius's fourth wife, Agrippina, who wanted him to tutor her son Nero. When Nero became emperor in 54 AD, Seneca at first helped him provide competent government. His influence declined with time, and in 65 AD Seneca was forced to take his own life for alleged complicity in a conspiracy to assassinate Nero; he was probably innocent. His stoic and calm suicide has become the subject of numerous paintings.

Stoics believed the fear of death to be a major challenge or test in every human life and, when Nero instructed him to commit suicide, Seneca followed Roman tradition by severing several veins in his arms in order to bleed to death, his wife following suit. A generation later, Tacitus wrote a somewhat saccharine account, according to which Nero ordered Seneca's wife saved. Her wounds were bound up and she made no further attempt to kill herself. As for Seneca himself, age and diet were blamed for the slow loss of blood and extended pain he suffered in lieu of a quick death. He next took hemlock, which however also failed to dispatch him. After dictating his last words to a scribe, and with a circle of friends attending him, he immersed himself in a warm bath, which he expected would speed blood flow and ease his pain. Tacitus tells us that the steam helped suffocate him. Seneca was burnt without any of the usual funeral rites as he had directed in a codicil of his will.

Together with Seneca's apparent fortitude in the face of death, his actions may also be seen as a tinge theatrical. The choice of hemlock as poison, and the decision alike to invite an audience of friends, both deliberately and perhaps hubristically recall Socrates's passing; at the same time the astonishing wealth Seneca had accumulated complicates the image Seneca might have liked of himself as ascetic. Nonetheless Seneca's influence persists today: 'to be philosophical' or 'take life philosophically' both imply a certain Duke of Edinburgh-style courage and steadfastness, even now.

A FATHER'S GRIEF IN *BEOWULF*

A most moving passage in *Beowulf* describes the grief of an old man, one of whose sons had been accidentally killed by his brother, so that the father has no way of avenging him. This is Seamus Heaney's translation:

> That offence was beyond redress, a wrongfooting
> Of the heart's affections; for who could avenge
> The prince's life or pay his death-price?
> It was like the misery endured by an old man
> Who has lived to see his son's body
> Swing on the gallows. He begins to keen
> And weep for his boy, watching the ravens
> Gloat where he hangs: he can be of no help.
> The wisdom of age is worthless to him.
> Morning after morning, he wakes to remember
> That his child is gone; he has no interest
> In living on until another heir
> Is born in the hall, now that his first-born
> Has entered death's dominion for ever.
> He gazes sorrowfully at his son's dwelling,
> The banquet hall bereft of all delight,
> The windswept hearthstone; the horsemen are
>   sleeping,
> The warriors under ground; what was is no more.

No tunes from the harp, no cheer raised in the
  yard.
Alone with his longing, he lies down on his bed
And sings a lament; everything seems too large,
The steadings and the fields.

STOP ALL THE CLOCKS

Everyone who saw it remembers the devastating scene in *Four Weddings and a Funeral* when the actor John Hannah recites W.H. Auden's 'Funeral Blues', a poem Auden first intended as a satire on Fascism.

> Stop all the clocks, cut off the telephone,
> Prevent the dog from barking with a juicy bone.
> Silence the pianos and with muffled drum
> Bring out the coffin, let the mourners come.
>
> Let aeroplanes circle moaning overhead
> Scribbling on the sky the message He is Dead,
> Put crêpe bows round the white necks of the
>   public doves,
> Let the traffic policemen wear black cotton gloves.
>
> He was my North, my South, my East and West,
> My working week and my Sunday rest...

Despite Auden's re-writing of the final stanzas, remaining references to sky-writing, traffic policemen and 'public doves' still imply the ostentatious, populist, fake funeral a Mussolini or a Franco might expect. The intense power and truth-to-emotion of John Hannah's acting obliterated this origin and universalised the message. After the film came out, American sales of Auden's poetry catapaulted (it is said) by half a million, while a slim pamphlet cooked up fast by Faber in London containing ten Auden poems including 'Funeral Blues' sold 275,000.* The *Sun* newspaper launched a free reader offer. Grief sells, we might cynically say. It is certainly universal. The John Hannah character quips that his gay partner preferred funerals to weddings, because 'It is easier to get enthusiastic about a ceremony one has an outside chance of eventually being involved in.'

---

* The Faber pamphlet was entitled *Tell Me the Truth about Love*. Auden's American publisher, Random House, had lost interest in him to the extent of not wanting to publish the definitive edition of his works: see James Fenton in https://www.independent.co.uk/voices/four-weddings-and-a-circle-of-poetry-1439475.html and also https://www.bl.uk/20th-century-literature/articles/an-introduction-to-stop-all-the-clocks

One of the most popular elegies in English must surely be the song from *Cymbeline* (Act IV Scene ii):

> Fear no more the heat o' the sun,
> Nor the furious winter's rages;
> Thou thy worldly task hast done,
> Home art gone, and ta'en thy wages:
> Golden lads and girls all must,
> As chimney-sweepers, come to dust.
>
> Fear no more the frown o' the great;
> Thou art past the tyrant's stroke;
> Care no more to clothe and eat;
> To thee the reed is as the oak:
> The sceptre, learning, physic, must
> All follow this, and come to dust.
>
> Fear no more the lightning flash,
> Nor the all-dreaded thunder stone;
> Fear not slander, censure rash;
> Thou hast finished joy and moan:
> All lovers young, all lovers must
> Consign to thee, and come to dust.

No exorciser harm thee!
Nor no witchcraft charm thee!
Ghost unlaid forbear thee!
Nothing ill come near thee!
Quiet consummation have;
And renownèd be thy grave!

These have been called 'possibly the most resonant lyric lines Shakespeare ever composed'. This dirge quietens and consoles: the dead are portrayed as enjoying final respite. We're invited to celebrate the fact that they have transcended extremes of heat and cold, are indifferent to the anxieties involved in finding food or clothing, have become immune to hardships such as bullying by tyrants or disfavour. Kings, scholars and doctors, like the humblest citizens (chimney sweeps), have all equally to face mortality.

The dead person has fulfilled the contract of life: just as a labourer returns home after being paid, so death is conceived of as home-coming. 'Home art gone and ta'en thy wages.' The implication is that the dead are now at peace. This elegy from *Cymbeline* is pastoral in the sense of idyllic; and this despite being sung by mistake – as it were – over the headless body of Cloten, a fool mistaken for the heroine's husband.

That Shakespeare knows grief has other faces is clear. Dying might be prettified as a home-coming; but mourners may also perceive it as a brutal exile. As Benedick puts it in *Much Ado* (Act III Scene ii), 'Everyone can master a grief but he that has it.' Mourning can also be aped and exaggerated. Hamlet refuses to stop wearing black at the start of the play of that name, using mourning dress to provoke his mother and uncle into remembering the murder of his father. Gertrude wisely but impotently protests that death is a universal fate: 'All that lives must die,/Passing through nature to eternity.'

In 1596 Shakespeare's 11-year-old son Hamnet died; probably while he was writing *King John*, a play also much concerned with grief over the unseasonable death of a son. Though nowadays the play has fallen out of fashion, Victorian audiences liked it, apparently tolerating the prodigious lamentations of Constance, widow of King John's elder brother, for her son Arthur, whose right to the throne she champions. That Arthur is still – unbeknownst to her – alive does not help her win the modern audience's sympathy. After pages of rhetorical display, Constance shares a recognisable description of how absence repeatedly triggers grief, one in which some have chosen to hear Shakespeare's experience:

> Grief fills the room up of my absent child.
> Lies in his bed, walks up and down with me.
> Puts on his pretty looks, repeats his words.
> Remembers me of all his gracious parts.
> Stuffs out his vacant garments with his form.
> Then, have I reason to be fond of grief.
>
> Act III Scene iv

King Philip of France, in front of whom she is performing, aptly comments, 'You are as fond of grief as of your child'; and one modern critic calls Constance 'an appalling woman'.

Her lament contrasts with two of the most powerful moments in Shakespeare's *oeuvre*, in both of which it is precisely the mourner's inarticulacy that moves us: the inability to find the right words, or any words at all, or a fixation on a horrified and uncomprehending repetition of a single word – in the case of Lear's speech below, 'never'. Cradling his dead daughter Cordelia, he protests:

> No, no, no life?
> Why should a dog, a horse, a rat have life,
> And thou no breath at all? Oh, thou'lt come
>   no more,
> Never, never, never, never, never.—
> Pray you, undo this button. Thank you, sir.
> Do you see this? Look on her. Look, her lips.
> Look there, look there. O, O, O, O. (*dies*)
>   Act V Scene iii

A moment of comparable power comes in *Macbeth* when Macduff struggles to apprehend the news that Macbeth has had his wife and all his children put to death. He repeats questions as if trying to digest the truth. 'My children too? ... My wife killed too? ... All my pretty ones?/Did you say all? ... All?/What, all my pretty chickens and their dam/At one fell swoop?' (the first usage of this phrase). And then, most memorably and most powerfully, when charged to 'Dispute it like a man' – i.e. to take his revenge – Macduff answers, 'I shall do so,/But I must also feel it as a man.'

This exchange suggests that real manhood is more than just aggression and murder; allowing oneself to be sensitive and feel grief is required. The passage runs:

ROSS: Your castle is surprised; your wife and
  babes
Savagely slaughter'd: to relate the manner,
Were, on the quarry of these murder'd deer,
To add the death of you.

MALCOLM: Merciful heaven!
What, man! ne'er pull your hat upon your brows;
Give sorrow words: the grief that does not speak
Whispers the o'er-fraught heart and bids it break.

MACDUFF: My children too?

ROSS: Wife, children, servants, all
That could be found.

MACDUFF: And I must be from thence!
My wife kill'd too?

ROSS: I have said.

MALCOLM: Be comforted:
Let's make us medicines of our great revenge,
To cure this deadly grief.

MACDUFF: He has no children. All my pretty
  ones?
Did you say all? O hell-kite! All?
What, all my pretty chickens and their dam
At one fell swoop?

MALCOLM: Dispute it like a man.

MACDUFF: I shall do so;
But I must also feel it as a man.

Act IV Scene iii

Shakespeare died – aged 52 – on 23 April 1616. One month before, he had signed his will, in which he describes himself as 'in perfect health'. No contemporary source explains how or why he died. Half a century later the vicar of Stratford noted that Shakespeare, Drayton and Ben Jonson had a merry meeting and, it seems, drank too hard, 'for Shakespeare died of a fever there contracted'. Of the tributes from fellow authors, one refers to his relatively sudden demise: 'We wondered, Shakespeare, that thou went'st so soon /From the world's stage to the grave's tiring room.'

One of the smallest tasks of bereavement can also be among the most harrowing: what to do with the clothes of the dead. The final words of Virginia Woolf's 1922 novel *Jacob's Room* concern the young, dead soldier's empty boots. Jacob's mother asks, ' "What am I to do with these, Mr. Bonamy?" She held out a pair of Jacob's old shoes.'

In her recent novel *Hamnet*, Maggie O'Farrell picks up and expands on this theme. In 1596 Shakespeare's son Hamnet died, aged 11; four years later came the first performances of *Hamlet*, an alternative spelling at that period of the same name. O'Farrell explores this confluence of names and events, ending with one hundred remarkable pages of Hamnet's mother's lamentations. One moving and disturbing passage follows:

> It is hard to know what to do with his clothes. For weeks, Agnes cannot move them from the chair where he left them before taking to bed. A month or so after the burial she lifts the breeches, then puts them down. She fingers the collar of his shirt. She nudges the toe of his boot so that the pair are lined up, side by side.
>
> Then she buries her face in the shirt; she presses the breeches to her heart; she inserts a hand into each

boot, feeling the empty shapes of his feet; she ties and unties the necklines; she pushes buttons into holes and out again. She folds the clothes, unfolds them, refolds them.

As the fabric runs through her fingers, as she puts each seam together, as she flaps out the creases in the air, her body remembers this task. It takes her back to the before. Folding his clothes, tending to them, breathing in his scent, she can almost persuade herself that he is still here, just about to get dressed, that he will walk through the door at any moment, asking, Wherever are my stockings, where is my shirt ?, worrying about being late for the school bell.

The many epigrams by Martial, a Roman poet from Spain, were published between AD 86 and 103. He often satirises city life, mocks his contemporaries and employs wit to celebrate immorality – resorting to insulting or obscene language. Yet he could also express humanity and love, most notably in the three poems he wrote about his little slave girl Erotion who died six days before her sixth birthday. He evidently loved her tenderly. In 5.37 he records her charm, and attacks a man who chides Martial for mourning a mere, little home-born slave. In 10.61 he asks future managers of his lands to preserve her grave; while in the poem that follows here (5.34), he urges his own deceased parents to help protect her in the realm of death.

> To you, my parents, I send on
> This little girl, Erotion,
> The slave I loved, that by your side
> Her ghost need not be terrified
> Of the pitch darkness underground
> Or the great jaws of Hades' hound.
> This winter she would have completed
> Her sixth year had she not been cheated
> By just six days. Lisping my name
> May she continue the sweet game

Of childhood happily down there
In two such good, old spirits' care.
Lie lightly on her, turf and dew,
She put so little weight on you.

SOMERSET MAUGHAM: LAST WORDS

'Dying is a very dull, dreary affair,' said Somerset Maugham to his nephew Robin Maugham, shortly before his death in 1965. 'And my advice to you is to have nothing whatever to do with it.'

'To lament that we shall not be alive a hundred years hence, is the same folly as to be sorry we were not alive a hundred years ago.'

Voltaire thought Michel de Montaigne (1533–92) wise. Emerson called him 'this prince of egotists... this admirable gossip'. Virginia Woolf admired him as a 'great master of the art of life'; while the *New Yorker* recently championed him as 'the first modern man'.

In 1571, aged 38, Michel de Montaigne retired from public life into the library he made within a tower of his family castle near Bordeaux, to spend much of the second half of his life exploring his own nature and in so doing inventing the modern form of the essay. (In French *essai* means trial or attempt.)

He enjoyed income from a large estate, and a fortune built on the salt-herring and wine trades, which had turned his family into landed gentry. Montaigne loved paradox, calling himself – 'bashful, insolent; chaste, lustful; prating, silent; laborious, delicate; ingenious, heavy; melancholic, pleasant; lying, true; knowing, ignorant; liberal, covetous, and prodigal'. 'I am myself the matter of my book,' he wrote. How should you live, and how should you die, he inquired? You should live in the present, at peace with yourself, free from vanity and anxiety, he seems to answer. He explored the virtues and the passions, fear, anger, witchcraft, smells, repentance... But his investigations are provisional and unstable, his imagination 'like a runaway horse'. He sees both sides of each question, embraces contradiction and is famously open to every kind of speculation, from the waywardness of penises – which have a mind and a will entirely of their own – to his fine celebrations of poetry and of conversation, of books (especially the classics) – and of friendship. His reflections attracted the attention of the Inquisition in Rome, and were translated into English by John Florio in 1603. Shakespeare exploited Montaigne both in *King Lear*, when Edmund perverts his thoughts on father–son relations, and in the *Tempest* when Gonzalo proposes an ideal commonwealth, borrowing from Montaigne's 'On the Cannibals'. He has been called a gentleman ethnographer, enchanted by the bewildering variety of human practices.

He was born and remained a Catholic Royalist while his mother and one brother converted and became Protestant. But he stayed on good terms with all factions. Appointed Gentleman to the Bedchamber to Catholic King Charles IX (1550–74), he was nonetheless also a close friend and confidant of the Protestant Henri de Navarre: he went on to serve as Navarre's emissary to the Catholic court of Charles's brother and successor, Henri III (1574–89). Montaigne lived through the eight terrible French wars of religion during which up to three million perished. He endured plague, too: in 1585, while he was mayor of Bordeaux, 14,000 citizens died – one third of the population of the city. The age provided many reminders of the importance of the question of how to die.

One early essay is entitled 'To philosophise is to learn how to die' while a late one, 'On Vanity', extends this same theme. Death and dying interested him, constituting the 'greatest human task'. Of his six daughters, five died in infancy, only one surviving to adulthood. Montaigne's good-natured, *sportif* brother Arnaud, an army captain, was felled by a blow from a tennis-ball just above the right ear. Five or six hours later he had a fit and died, aged only 23. This freak accident horrified Montaigne, who soon suffered further bereavements. His best-beloved, most intimate friend and soul-mate, the poet Etienne de La Boétie, died bravely and in agony, of dysentery (possibly plague) in 1563, still holding forth. Next, his father died of a kidney-stone attack. 'With such frequent and ordinary examples passing before our eyes,' he wrote, 'how can we possibly rid ourselves of the thought of death and of the idea that at every moment it is gripping us by the throat?' Death, he thought, is when you discover who you truly are.

As Montaigne rode out one day to the forests near his home, a faster rider collided with him, sending him flying from his horse. He landed metres away, knocked out. He came to, groggily, while being carried home by his companions – who later told him that he was vomiting blood and clawing at his chest violently, as if to tear himself from his body. Yet his inner experiences were entirely different. He recalled floating on a cloud of euphoria, as if sweetly drifting off to sleep. This sense of well-being faded only when he returned to full consciousness, and to experience the pain of his injuries. The episode modified his view of death and dying: we have nothing to fear but fear itself, he was the first person to note, three centuries before Roosevelt.

'To practise death is to practise freedom,' he reflected. 'A man who has learned how to die has unlearned how to be a slave. Knowing how to die gives us freedom from subjection and constraint.' That is, freedom from fear, as also from excessive grief, which was regarded by Stoics as a destructive passion. So his thinking about grief links him to Seneca and the ancient world, while yet making him into our contemporary too: grief is to be eschewed, forgone. We are invited to be sceptical of its value. This suggests a wise and pragmatic bravery that might still be serviceable today.

He doubts the doctrine of immortality and has a special horror of the apparatus surrounding dying – and especially of the contagious and upsetting distress of survivors. 'If I were allowed to choose I would, I think, prefer to die in the saddle rather than in my bed, away from home and far from my own folk. There is more heartbreak than comfort in taking leave of those we love... I would willingly therefore neglect to bid that great and everlasting farewell... A man should diffuse joy but, as much as he can, smother grief.' He returns to this theme with great eloquence and force in 'On Vanity'. Dying should ideally happen quietly and among strangers.

Diffusing joy Montaigne was adept at; he was no solitary recluse. In truth, he went to the best parties, attended society weddings and had everybody's ear. 'He corresponded with beautiful, educated women who read his drafts. He dined at the castle with well-born men who had learned to value his advice and diplomacy during his years of "public duties".'* He left his tower in 1580 for one year of passion-

---

* Jane Kramer 'Me, myself and I: What made Michel de Montaigne the first modern man', *New Yorker*, 31 August 2009.

73

ate travelling; and left it again in 1581 to become mayor of Bordeaux. Two years later, he agreed to a second term. His search for the spa that would cure his kidney stones took him to Switzerland, Austria, and Germany. His love of the classics took him to Rome, where he kissed the slippers of the Pope and was made an honorary Roman citizen.

He did not a achieve the quiet, grief-free and anonymous death among strangers he so desired. Instead he died of quinsy (an abscess of the tonsils) at the age of 59, in 1592. This disease paralysed his tongue, an especially horrible fate for one who once said, 'the most fruitful and natural play of the mind is conversation' and who recorded that he would rather lose his sight than his hearing or voice. Remaining in possession of all his other faculties – and despite his scepticism about the life to come – he requested Mass. He died in his room during its celebration.

THE HORSES OF ACHILLES

A short episode of the *Iliad* Book 17 concerns two immortal horses – named Balius and Xanthus[*] – given as a wedding-gift to Peleus and his sea-nymph bride. Heroic Achilles, the son of this particular union, uses them to drive his chariot during the Trojan War; while his beloved soul-mate and comrade-in-arms Patroclus feeds and grooms them. And only Patroclus is able fully to control them: they are described as able to fly 'like the wind'. When Patroclus is killed in battle, Xanthus and Balius stand motionless on the field of battle and weep.

> The horses... stood out of the fight and wept when they heard that their driver had been laid low by the hand of murderous Hector. Automedon... lashed them again and again; many a time did he speak kindly to them, and many a time did he upbraid them, but they would neither go back to the ships by the waters of the broad Hellespont, nor yet into battle among the Achaeans; they stood with their chariot stock still, as a pillar set over the tomb of some dead man or woman, and bowed their heads to the ground. Hot tears fell from their eyes as they mourned the loss of their

[*] With Pedasos a possible third – but mortal – mentioned in *Iliad* Book 16.

charioteer, and their noble manes drooped all wet from under the yoke straps on either side the yoke.

The son of Saturn [Zeus] saw them and took pity upon their sorrow. He wagged his head, and muttered to himself, saying, 'Poor things, why did we give you to King Peleus who is a mortal, while you are yourselves ageless and immortal? Was it that you might share the sorrows that befall mankind? For of all creatures that live and move upon the earth there is none so pitiable as he is—.'

The pathos surrounding the horses of Achilles is central to our sense of the *Iliad* as tragic as well as epic. It is *grief itself*, rather like the horses, that is immortal. The number of heroic, individual, named warriors in the poem whose deaths we witness is around 318. Homer's strange trope underwrites the futility of war and the defencelessness of all human life. The episode has attracted the attention of painters – Anthony van Dyck, de Chirico – as also of writers – Constantine Cavafy, Iris Murdoch. Cavafy's poem bespeaks what he calls 'the eternal disaster of human death'. As for Achilles, he gets his revenge when he kills his arch-enemy Hector, whose father Priam, in another memorable scene, weeps as he begs for his son's body for burial. Achilles weeps with him, and for the common fate of all men.

T.S. ELIOT: 'LITTLE GIDDING'

T.S. Eliot served as an air raid warden walking the streets of Kensington during the Second World War. He published 'Little Gidding', the fourth and final section of his *Four Quartets*, with its momentous summary line 'History is now and England', in 1942. The Blitz had delayed publication by one year. As with Dylan Thomas's poem 'A Refusal to Mourn the Death, by Fire, of a Child in London', readers welcomed the poet's struggle to meditate in public on shared disaster.

> What the dead had no speech for, when living
> They can tell you being dead: the communication
> Of the dead is tongued with fire beyond the
>   language of the living.
> Here, the intersection of the timeless moment
> Is England and nowhere. Never and always.

EDNA ST VINCENT MILLAY: 'TIME DOES NOT BRING RELIEF'

This sonnet by Edna St Vincent Millay (1892–1950) may be thought prophetic: it was published early in her career, during the year that she graduated from Vassar College in 1917, and thus before she had properly embarked on a colourful career that would encompass a reputation as a daring bohemian, the 1923 Pulitzer Prize for Poetry, and 11 collections of verse including 170 sonnets. She was a socialist and patriotic propagandist against Fascism before and during the Second World War. Her sonnet 'Time does not bring relief' laments the pain of loss. Her parents died in the 1930s and her husband in 1949 after surgery for lung cancer. Millay, who with her husband often drank to excess, suffered a brief and inconsolable widowhood, dying alone at her home in New York state after falling on her staircase.

> Time does not bring relief; you all have lied
> Who told me time would ease me of my pain!
> I miss him in the weeping of the rain;
> I want him at the shrinking of the tide;
> The old snows melt from every mountain-side,
> And last year's leaves are smoke in every lane;
> But last year's bitter loving must remain
> Heaped on my heart, and my old thoughts abide.

There are a hundred places where I fear
To go,—so with his memory they brim.
And entering with relief some quiet place
Where never fell his foot or shone his face
I say, 'There is no memory of him here!'
And so stand stricken, so remembering him.

Among 14,000 surviving letters by the great Austrian poet Rainer Maria Rilke (1875–1926) are two dozen addressed to bereaved friends; these were published in 2018 as *The Dark Interval: Letters for the Grieving Heart.*

Letters of condolence are notoriously hard to pen. We fumble for something that might help, share memories, hope that time heals. Rilke's certainty that he has something of value to offer is strikingly different. He believes that 'time itself does not console, as people say superficially' – and nor does he offer cheap promises about the afterlife: 'I do not love the Christian idea of a Beyond.' Death is nevertheless among his special subjects, and he knows how lonely survival can be.

One letter memorably evokes the indescribably desolate state of an abandoned small child as an analogue of bereavement. And he maintains that we should not aspire to being consoled but develop curiosity instead about exploring loss as our new inner landscape.

Rilke puts the highest value on loneliness. In his *Letters to a Young Poet* (published in 1929), he stressed the central importance of solitude and unflinching self-reckoning, arguing that we must come to understand that our fragile inner world – which will perforce always encompass pain and uncertainty – is our central resource. This inner world constitutes our wealth; and attention (or as we might say today, 'mindfulness'), which he valued highly, could unlock it. In one wonderful letter he commented that, when Cezanne painted a particular self-portrait, he watched *not as a human being watches, but as a dog watches*. Rilke believed that close attention and not turning away can also help on the lonely journey of grieving.

He himself attended generously and lovingly. He brooded patiently upon each friend's needs. Very different letters start alike: 'I would like to be with you in response'; 'I am so very moved that I want to extend my hands to you'; and 'I have read [your letter] again and again, to be close to you and to completely understand and to grasp the current condition of your pain.' 'I read your letter with attentiveness and joy.'

This practice of loving attention paid off: and his letters, evidently treasured, survived. He felt a deep need to reach out and impart wisdom; and though he never offers any quick fix or panacea, common themes emerge. As Kate Kellaway has put this: 'His conviction was that we must not turn away from death. The focus must be absolute. But he also dwells on the way death throws life into sharper relief. We can, he believes, live more intensely because of it.'

Rilke's attitude resembles that of a mystic, in that it is both worldly and other-worldly. On the one hand, he emphasises that grief is hard physical labour: 'Not one person has been taken from me without my having found the tasks around me increased.' On the other, he pleads for a change of heart and a transfiguration of the ordinary. Grief, manifesting often as an 'impoverishing daily bitterness', has other, hidden dimensions too, just like the moon, [with] a side that is permanently turned away from us...'. 'I do not mean that we should love death... but love life so generously and without calculation that one always includes it... in one's love too.'

A loving attention, as for other mystics, provokes the wholeness that death appears to shatter, going beyond dualism itself. He recalls once having listened to a bird call on Capri: it forced him to close his eyes and seemed to be 'both outside and inside him'. No accident that he wrote three poems to the Buddha, who also preached going beyond duality. To go beyond would mean entering what Rilke calls 'an open world', where 'openness' seems to point towards egolessness. He knows that nobody comes close to true assistance and consolation 'except by an act of grace'.

Ultimately, Rilke urges a healing surrender to the sheer contingency of existence, a saying 'Yes' to life that is neither Pollyanna-ish, nor easy. 'Even despair is a kind of abundance,' he proclaims, and 'when things become truly difficult and unbearable, we find ourselves in a place close to transformation.'

He died of leukaemia in the arms of his doctor in a sanatorium in Switzerland, on 29 December 1926, aged 51, troubled by ulcerous sores in his mouth, stomach-pains and low spirits. It is recorded that he was 'open-eyed'. His poem 'Death' reads:

> Before us great Death stands
> Our fate held close within his quiet hands.
> When with proud joy we lift Life's red wine
> To drink deep of the mystic shining cup

And ecstasy through all our being leaps—
Death bows his head and weeps.

Jean Jacques Rousseau, in his epistolary novel *Julie, or the New Eloise*, published in Amsterdam in 1761, made no bones about the idea of fearing death, and showed that there should be no shame in it: 'He who pretends to look on death without fear lies. All men are afraid of dying, this is the great law of sentient beings, without which the entire human species would soon be destroyed.'

BEN JONSON: 'ON MY FIRST SON'

In this moving testament to his anguish and grief in the wake of his son's death, Jonson wrestles with some of the toughest questions a poet – and a person – can face. He asks himself whether he can ever recover from such a sharp blow – and he wonders whether anything can possibly compensate for his loss.

On My First Son

Farewell, thou child of my right hand, and joy;
My sin was too much hope of thee, lov'd boy.
Seven years thou wert lent to me, and I thee pay,
Exacted by thy fate, on the just day.
O, could I lose all father now! For why
Will man lament the state he should envy?
To have so soon 'scap'd world's and flesh's rage,
And if no other misery, yet age?
Rest in soft peace, and, ask'd, say, 'Here doth lie
Ben Jonson his best piece of poetry.'
For whose sake henceforth all his vows be such,
As what he loves may never like too much.

In Memoriam is a requiem written by Alfred Lord Tennyson for his close friend Henry Hallam, who had died suddenly of apoplexy aged only 22 in Vienna. Seventeen years in the making, divided into 133 Cantos or 723 stanzas, it ranks among the longest elegies in English. It begins with a funeral, ends with a marriage, and in between evokes the life-journey of bereavement.

One original title was 'The Way of the Soul'; and the poem interrogates our shared condition of mortality and grief. Queen Victoria kept a copy on her bedside table together with her Bible. It 'soothed and pleased' her during the four long decades of widowhood that followed Albert's death in 1861. She met the poet twice. At Osborne on the Isle of Wight in April 1862, she recorded: 'I went down to see Tennyson who is very peculiar looking, tall, dark, with a fine head, long black flowing hair and a beard – oddly dressed, but there is no affectation about him. I told him how much I admired his glorious lines to my precious Albert and how much comfort I found in his *In Memoriam*.'

After a period in limbo, *In Memoriam* has found new audiences and admirers. Its enduring power lies less today in its affirmations of rediscovered faith than in its wonderfully lyrical explorations of desolation and despair; and its proclamation that 'There lives more faith in honest doubt,/Believe me, than in half the creeds.' Poet and friend Edward Fitzgerald commented that if Tennyson had got on a horse and ridden twenty miles 'instead of moaning over his pipe, he would have been cured of his sorrows in half the time.' But for Tennyson poetry was the best location in which to digest the darkest of views: indeed, the topic of suicide appears in many Tennyson poems over the years.

One early stanza evokes the poet's sadness at his own survival as something at once physical and atmospheric.

> Dark house, by which once more I stand
>> Here in the long unlovely street,
>> Doors, where my heart was used to beat
> So quickly, waiting for a hand,
>
> A hand that can be clasp'd no more—
>> Behold me, for I cannot sleep,
>> And like a guilty thing I creep
> At earliest morning to the door.
>
> He is not here; but far away
>> The noise of life begins again,
>> And ghastly thro' the drizzling rain
> On the bald street breaks the blank day.

The alliteration within the final line of its three b-words – bald, breaks and blank – accentuates its bleakness. Bad news inspires Tennyson to write powerful verse. It also causes him to question his own religious faith and suffer the uncertainty that followed. He referred late in life to the 'terrible muses' of astronomy and geology that dwarf and

humble the human life-span; and indeed he evokes the un-
imaginability of geological time in verses of matchless beauty and wonder.

> There rolls the deep where grew the tree.
>   O earth, what changes hast thou seen!
>   There where the long street roars, hath been
> The stillness of the central sea.
>
> The hills are shadows, and they flow
>   From form to form, and nothing stands;
>   They melt like mist, the solid lands,
> Like clouds they shape themselves and go.
>
> But in my spirit will I dwell,
>   And dream my dream, and hold it true;
>   For tho' my lips may breathe adieu,
> I cannot think the thing farewell.

A further 'terrible muse' was to be found in the new biol-
ogy that demonstrated the interconnectedness of all living
forms, and prompted Tennyson to fearfully compare the
value of human life to that of flies that 'lay their eggs and
sting'. Canto 50 has the form of a prayer addressed to Hallam's spirit, requesting his comfort and reassurance when
possessed by such fears.

> Be near me when my light is low,
> When the blood creeps, and the nerves prick
> And tingle; and the heart is sick,
> And all the wheels of Being slow.

Be near me when the sensuous frame
Is rack'd with pangs that conquer trust;
And Time, a maniac scattering dust,
And Life, a fury slinging flame.

Be near me when my faith is dry,
And men the flies of latter spring,
That lay their eggs, and sting and sing
And weave their petty cells and die.

Be near me when I fade away,
To point the term of human strife,
And on the low dark verge of life
The twilight of eternal day.

If the essence of this great and sprawling poem had to be reduced to a couplet this might well be ' 'Tis better to have loved and lost/Than never to have loved at all.' That loss is built into love does not empty it of value; in a sense it stands as guarantor of that value. Tennyson returned memorably to his chosen theme of loss in his elegiac 'Crossing the Bar', written in October 1889 while crossing the Solent: this time future loss. It concerns Canto 50's 'low dark verge of life' and expresses his hope of travelling calmly and securely through death to meet God (the 'Pilot') face to face. His son when shown this poem said, 'That is the crown of your life's work.' Tennyson answered, 'It came in a moment.' Death is conceived of as home-coming.

Sunset and evening star,
    And one clear call for me!

And may there be no moaning of the bar,
  When I put out to sea,

But such a tide as moving seems asleep,
  Too full for sound and foam,
When that which drew from out the boundless deep
  Turns again home.

Twilight and evening bell,
  And after that the dark!
And may there be no sadness of farewell,
  When I embark;

For tho' from out our bourne of Time and Place
  The flood may bear me far,
I hope to see my Pilot face to face
  When I have crost the bar.

DOMESTICATING GRIEF: EMILY DICKINSON

In many dark poems Emily Dickinson tests the fierce Calvinist faith she was brought up in, with its promises of the afterlife, and its threats of hell. In others she domesticates death, seeing in grief new chores for survivors. Dickinson, who famously never married and did not leave her Amherst home for 15 years, grew accustomed to regular housework. In her wonderful 'Aftermath' (probably from 1866) she compares the job of grief itself – by implication – to a specialised form of housekeeping. Grief-work, as it were, means 'sweeping up the heart,/And putting love away'. Domesticating grief has here the side-effect of showing how, with time, it gets distanced.

Aftermath

The bustle in a house
The morning after death
Is solemnest of industries
Enacted upon earth,

The sweeping up the heart,
And putting love away
We shall not want to use again
Until eternity.

Unlike, say, Wilfred Owen, who would later paint death as a comrade-at-arms in the Trenches – 'Oh, Death was never enemy of ours!/We laughed at him, we leagued with him, old chum' – Dickinson (despite living through the carnage of the Civil War) locates death mostly within the home, where she herself witnessed dying. Much obsessed by death, she always seeks out a strange angle of vision to render her subject-matter accessible yet also mysterious in the same instant. Over one third of her 1,500 poems address mortality; and domestication implies familiarity.

Her poems tend to advertise being on easy terms with mortality. So two sorts of intimacy jostle in her epitaphs while she introduces death and the reader, the one to the other. Here grief causes absence and loss, yet is also haunted by presence, recalling the waxing and waning of the moon, or the cyclical movement of tides.

> Each that we lose takes part of us;
> A crescent still abides,
> Which like the moon, some turbid night,
> Is summoned by the tides.

Dickinson's tone is informal, her punctuation – which often includes many dashes – miming the movement of thought itself.

> Because I could not stop for Death –
> He kindly stopped for me –
> The Carriage held but just Ourselves –
> And Immortality.
> We slowly drove – He knew no haste

And I had put away
My labor and my leisure too,
For His Civility –

We passed the School, where Children strove
At Recess – in the Ring –
We passed the Fields of Gazing Grain –
We passed the Setting Sun –

Or rather – He passed Us –
The Dews drew quivering and Chill –
For only Gossamer, my Gown –
My Tippet – only Tulle –

We paused before a House that seemed
A Swelling of the Ground –
The Roof was scarcely visible –
The Cornice – in the Ground –

Since then – 'tis Centuries – and yet
Feels shorter than the Day
I first surmised the Horses' Heads
Were toward Eternity –

Death in these verses is a gentleman manifesting 'civility', kindly stopping his carriage for the poet to invite her on a journey that is both pedestrian – with its passing schoolchildren and evocations of the evening – and also startling and uncanny, in that a living poet hints throughout at apprehending the long perspectives of 'Eternity'.

Dickinson is adept at disguising what she really feels

behind a mask of apparent reticence and nonchalance, a capacity sometimes called *sprezzatura*. This form of defensive irony or brave performance-art invokes a courage that that might be aped in a poem, or lived, too. The difficult action about which Dickinson teases is dying. She wrote many epitaphs and most are enigmatic, not least when, as in 'I heard a Fly buzz', she once again envisages her own end.

I heard a Fly buzz – when I died –
The Stillness in the Room
Was like the Stillness in the Air –
Between the Heaves of Storm –

The Eyes around – had wrung them dry –
And Breaths were gathering firm
For that last Onset – when the King
Be witnessed – in the Room –

I willed my Keepsakes – Signed away
What portion of me be
Assignable – and then it was
There interposed a Fly –

With Blue – uncertain – stumbling Buzz –
Between the light – and me –
And then the Windows failed – and then
I could not see to see –

As for the business of grief, Dickinson knew how moments of intense suffering can be followed by bouts of inactivity, paralysis or numbness: she understood that lack of feeling is as much a feature of the grieving process as deeply felt pain:

> After great pain, a formal feeling comes –
> The Nerves sit ceremonious, like Tombs –
> The stiff Heart questions 'was it He, that bore,'
> And 'Yesterday, or Centuries before'?
>
> The Feet, mechanical, go round –
> A Wooden way
> Of Ground, or Air, or Ought –
> Regardless grown,
> A Quartz contentment, like a stone –
>
> This is the Hour of Lead –
> Remembered, if outlived,
> As Freezing persons, recollect the Snow –
> First – Chill – then Stupor – then the letting go –

She died, probably of Bright's disease, on 15 May 1886 after two and a half years of ill health. Her white-garbed body lay in a white coffin. The pallbearers, among them the president and professors of Amherst College, set the casket down after exiting the Homestead's back door, and their burden was shouldered, at the poet's own request, by six Irish workmen who had been hired men on the Dickinson grounds.

Following her directions, they circled her flower garden, walked through the great barn that stood behind the house, and took a grassy path across house lots and fields of buttercups to West Cemetery, followed by the friends who had attended the simple service. There Emily Dickinson was interred in a grave lined with evergreen boughs, within the family plot enclosed by an iron fence.

ALAN TURING: THE COUNTER-INTUITIVE REALITY OF 'ALIVENESS'

When he was 20 Alan Turing's great friend – the love of his life – Christopher Morcom died of a chance infection. Turing, in letters to Christopher's mother from April 1933, articulated a vision of the world that rejected the predetermined and made a secure place for 'spirit' and the counter-intuitive reality of 'aliveness'.

> I was so pleased to be at the Clockhouse for Easter. I always like to think of it specially in connection with Chris. It reminds us that Chris is in some way alive *now*. One is perhaps too inclined to think only of him alive at some future time when we shall meet him again; but it is really so much more helpful to think of him as just separated from us for the present...
>
> [...]It used to be supposed in Science that if everything was known about the Universe at any particular moment then we can predict what it will be through all the future. ... More modern science however has come to the conclusion that when we are dealing with atoms and electrons we are quite unable to know the exact state of them; our instruments being made of atoms and electrons themselves.
>
> [...]Then as regards the actual connection be-

tween spirit and body I consider that the body by reason of being a living body can attract and hold on to a 'spirit' whilst the body is alive and awake and the two are firmly connected. When the body is asleep I cannot guess what happens but when the body dies the 'mechanism' of the body, holding the spirit, is gone and the spirit finds a new body sooner or later perhaps immediately.

As regards the question of why we have bodies at all; why we do not or cannot live free as spirits and communicate as such, we probably could do so but there would be nothing whatever to do. The body provides something for the spirit to look after and use.

Sir Arthur Conan Doyle, who created Sherlock Holmes, brilliant at solving mysteries and the most famous of all sleuths, was himself credulous. Around 1924 he wrote to an Irishwoman called Hester Travers Smith (1868–1949) requesting that she mention his name to Oscar Wilde.* Although Wilde had been dead for more than two decades, Smith had been receiving messages from him via a Ouija board, seances, and automatic writing sessions. She had recently published *Psychic Messages from Oscar Wilde*, winning herself money and fame and convincing Conan Doyle of the authenticity of these posthumous bulletins.

'If you are in contact [with Oscar],' Conan Doyle wrote, 'you might mention me to him – I knew him – and tell him that if he would honour me by coming through my wife who is an excellent automatic writer, there are some things which I should wish to say.' Wilde was evidently too busy at the time to attend properly to this request, instead dictating a posthumous play to Smith, appropriately entitled *Is it a Forgery?* Hester's spirit-guides included an ancient Egyptian priest, a Hindu and a Jewish neo-Platonist. They helpfully con-

---

* *TLS* , 24 January 2020, Annette Federico on *Beautiful Untrue Things: Forging Oscar Wilde's Extraordinary Afterlife* by G. Mackie (2019).

firmed that Shakespeare's works were indeed written either by Francis Bacon or by the Earl of Oxford, while revealing as an aside that Oberon in *A Midsummer Night's Dream* is the portrait of a bastard son of Elizabeth I.

Conan Doyle was not alone in being gullible: moreover it is hard nowadays to recapture how spiritualism once was regarded. In the USA, where the eminent philosopher William James was founding member and vice-president of the American Society for Psychical Research (SPR), and attended seances, spiritualism was often a 'progressive' cause, linked to the emancipation of women and (sometimes) the abolition of slavery. In Britain, Fellows of Trinity College, Cambridge took a leading role in the founding of the SPR, whose distinguished members included Arthur Balfour, philosopher and indeed Prime Minister from 1902–1905. After the slaughter of the First World War many hungered to communicate with their dead. Seances, mediums and Ouija boards abounded.

Conan Doyle in *Memories and Adventures* (1924) describes his grandmother's corpse as his first memory; and his interest in spiritualism went back to the previous century. He joined the Society for Psychical Research in 1893 and became a staunch advocate. He lost his brother-in-law Malcolm Leckie during the Battle of Mons in 1914 and then in the final days before the Armistice of 1918 lost his handsome eldest son Kingsley who had wanted to devote his life to medicine (like – initially – his father) and had started to study at St Mary's Hospital in London. When war broke out he interrupted his studies to serve in the army. 'One of the grandest boys in body and soul that ever a father was blessed with,' Doyle wrote. Kingsley was badly wounded by two shrapnel bullets in the neck on the Somme. Pneumonia killed him in London two years after. While Leckie communicated with Doyle post-mortem through automatic writing, blurred images of a face that Doyle claimed as Kingsley's appear in family photographs after his death. Then in 1918 Sir Arthur's brother General Innes Doyle died of pneumonia.

It has been pointed out that Conan Doyle's advocacy of spiritualism – the denial of death – won him some degree of peace amidst these pitiful losses. And he was by no means the only writer exercised by spiritualism. Rudyard Kipling, who lost his only son Jack at the Battle of Loos in 1915, a month after his eighteenth birthday, was interested in spiritualism, although he eventually decided it was psychologically dangerous: he held that his sister's long periods of mental illness were partly caused by the 'soul-destroying business of "spiritualism"' (letter, 3 June 1927). He was sceptical of the mediums who claimed to speak to or for the dead, and wrote a poem called 'En-dor' warning mothers against attempting to contact the men they had lost in the war, denouncing mediums as fraudsters and con-artists. 'And that those who have passed to the further shore/May' be hailed – at a price – on the road to En-dor' (a reference to the witch of Endor, consulted by Saul in the first Book of Samuel in the Old Testament to receive advice about tackling the Philistines in battle. Christian theologians were troubled by the implication that the witch summoned Samuel's spirit through necromancy or magic, and Kipling exploited this suspicion). He described his poem as 'A direct attack on the present mania of "Spiritualism" among such as have lost men during the war. It ought to be quoted extensively in the U.S. especially the third verse and the last. It will provoke a great deal of protest and discussion.'

Kipling died on 18 January 1936, his wedding anniversary, a few weeks after his seventieth birthday, having suffered a haemorrhage from a perforated ulcer. Cremated at Golders Green, his ashes were buried in Poets' Corner, Westminster Abbey.

En-Dor

'Behold there is a woman that
hath a familiar spirit at En-Dor.'
    I Samuel, xxviii, 7

The road to En-dor is easy to tread
For Mother or yearning Wife.
There, it is sure, we shall meet our Dead
As they were even in life.
Earth has not dreamed of the blessing in store
For desolate hearts on the road to En-dor.

Whispers shall comfort us out of the dark –
Hands – ah God! – that we knew!
Visions and voices – look and hark! –
Shall prove that the tale is true,
And that those who have passed to the further shore
May' be hailed – at a price – on the road to
  En-dor.

But they are so deep in their new eclipse
Nothing they say can reach,

Unless it be uttered by alien lips
And framed in a stranger's speech.
The son must send word to the mother that bore,
'Through an hireling's mouth. 'Tis the rule of
  En-dor.

And not for nothing these gifts are shown
By such as delight our dead.
They must twitch and stiffen and slaver and groan
Ere the eyes are set in the head,
And the voice from the belly begins. Therefore,
We pay them a wage where they ply at En-dor.

Even so, we have need of faith
And patience to follow the clue.
Often, at first, what the dear one saith
Is babble, or jest, or untrue.
(Lying spirits perplex us sore
Till our loves – and their lives – are well-known at
  En-dor). .

Oh the road to En-dor is the oldest road
And the craziest road of all!
Straight it runs to the Witch's abode,
As it did in the days of Saul,
And nothing has changed of the sorrow in store
For such as go down on the road to En-dor!

HENRY VAUGHAN: 'THEY ARE ALL GONE INTO THE WORLD OF LIGHT'

Possibly loneliness at the death of his first wife after 1650 prompted Vaughan to write this poem: the exact context is unknown. The first line summons the elegiac impulse and encompasses a personal *cri de coeur* with its final exclamation mark. Yet the poem celebrates loss and mourning as if they might be redemptive as much as tragic. The opening words, 'They are all', suggest impersonality and distance as much as intense communion: the reader is invited to join in a general act of mourning and to join an unseen congregation. Moreover, the ascended souls, seen 'walking in an air of glory', form a mystical vision. But this elevated rhetoric is qualified. Vaughan also – and almost casually – picks up spiritual images from the natural world he loves, such as the empty bird's-nest in stanza six, which domesticate his argument and bring it closer to us and the everyday.

'They are all gone into the world of light' belongs with Vaughan's other great visionary poems, all of which celebrate silence and solitude. 'The World' starts 'I saw eternity the other night/Like a great ring of pure and endless light' and 'The Night' show Vaughan finding within the hidden God Himself 'a deep but dazzling darkness', within which he aspires to 'live invisible and dim'.

Vaughan died aged 73 in Brecknockshire in 1695, on 23

April, like Shakespeare before him; the cause of his death unknown.

> They are all gone into the world of light!
> And I alone sit ling'ring here;
> Their very memory is fair and bright,
> And my sad thoughts doth clear.
>
> It glows and glitters in my cloudy breast,
> Like stars upon some gloomy grove,
> Or those faint beams in which this hill is drest,
> After the sun's remove.
>
> I see them walking in an air of glory,
> Whose light doth trample on my days:
> My days, which are at best but dull and hoary,
> Mere glimmering and decays.
>
> O holy Hope! and high Humility,
> High as the heavens above!
> These are your walks, and you have show'd them
>   me
> To kindle my cold love.
>
> Dear, beauteous Death! the jewel of the just,
> Shining nowhere, but in the dark;
> What mysteries do lie beyond thy dust
> Could man outlook that mark!
>
> He that hath found some fledg'd bird's nest, may
>   know

At first sight, if the bird be flown;
But what fair well or grove he sings in now,
That is to him unknown.

And yet as angels in some brighter dreams
Call to the soul, when man doth sleep:
So some strange thoughts transcend our wonted
  themes
And into glory peep.

If a star were confin'd into a tomb,
Her captive flames must needs burn there;
But when the hand that lock'd her up, gives room,
She'll shine through all the sphere.

O Father of eternal life, and all
Created glories under thee!
Resume thy spirit from this world of thrall
Into true liberty.

Either disperse these mists, which blot and fill
My perspective still as they pass,
Or else remove me hence unto that hill,
Where I shall need no glass.

FROM VERSES ON THE DEATH OF DR. SWIFT, BY JONATHAN SWIFT

In 1731, Jonathan Swift wrote to a friend, 'I have been several months writing near five hundred lines on a pleasant subject, only to tell what my friends and enemies will say on me after I am dead.' His poem meditates the truth of La Rochefoucauld's famously dark maxim that we find something not un-pleasing in the misfortunes of our friends. While the fun Swift makes out of human vanity is provocative, it also serves as a reminder that the topic of death need not be without comedy.

> Behold the fatal day arrive!
> 'How is the Dean?' – 'He's just alive.'
> Now the departing prayer is read;
> 'He hardly breathes.' – 'The Dean is dead.'
> Before the passing-bell begun,
> The news thro' half the town has run.
> 'O, may we all for death prepare!
> What has he left? and who's his heir?' –
> 'I know no more than what the news is;
> 'Tis all bequeath'd to public uses.' –
> 'To public use! a perfect whim!
> What had the public done for him?
> Mere envy, avarice, and pride:

He gave it all – but first he died.
And had the Dean, in all the nation,
No worthy friend, no poor relation?
So ready to do strangers good,
Forgetting his own flesh and blood?'

Now Grub-Street wits are all employ'd;
With elegies the town is cloy'd:
Some paragraph in ev'ry paper
To curse the Dean or bless the Drapier.

The doctors, tender of their fame,
Wisely on me lay all the blame:
'We must confess his case was nice;
But he would never take advice.
Had he been rul'd, for aught appears,
He might have liv'd these twenty years;
For, when we open'd him, we found
That all his vital parts were sound.'

DOUGLAS DUNN: THE 'GRIEF BEFORE THE GRIEF'

The Scottish poet Dunn's first collection, *Terry Street* (1969), deals more or less exclusively with observations of his home and immediate surroundings. This poem comes from the superb collection *Elegies* (1985), a sensitive (but not syrupy) commemoration of his late wife and celebration of her courage and grace. 'Grief before the grief' wonderfully evokes what might be called premonitory grief, that which we experience in anticipation.

Thirteen Steps and the Thirteenth of March

She sat up on her pillows, receiving guests.
I brought them tea or sherry like a butler,
Up and down the thirteen steps from my pantry.
I was running out of vases.

More than one visitor came down, and said,
'Her room's so cheerful. She isn't afraid.'
Even the cyclamen and lilies were listening,
Their trusty tributes holding off the real.

Doorbells, shopping, laundry, post and callers,

On Grief

And twenty-six steps up the stairs
From door to bed, two times thirteen's
Unlucky numeral in my high house.

And visitors, three, four, five times a day;
My wept exhaustions over plates and cups
Drained my self-pity in these days of grief
Before the grief. Flowers, and no vases left.

Tea, sherry, biscuits, cake and whisky for the
   weak…
She fought death with an understated mischief –
'I suppose I'll have to make an effort' –
Turning down the painkillers for lucidity.

Some sat downstairs with a hankie
Nursing a little cry before going up to her.
They came back with their fears of dying amended.
'Her room's so cheerful. She isn't afraid.'

Each day was duty round the clock.
Our kissing conversations kept me going,
Those times together with the phone switched off,
Remembering our lives by candlelight.

John and Stuart brought their pictures round,
A travelling exhibition. Dying,
She thumbed down some, nodded at others,
An artist and curator to the last,

Honesty at all costs. She drew up lists,

Bequests, gave things away. It tore my heart out.
Her friends assisted at this tidying
In a conspiracy of women.

At night, I lay beside her in the unique hours.
There were no mysteries in candle-shadows,
Birds, aeroplanes, the rabbits of our fingers,
The lovely, erotic flame of the candlelight.

Sad? Yes. But it was beautiful also.
There was a stillness in the world. Time was out
Walking his dog by the low walls and privet.
There was anonymity in words and music.

She wanted me to wear her wedding ring.
It wouldn't fit even my little finger.
It jammed on the knuckle. I knew why.
Her fingers dwindled and her rings slipped off.

After the funeral, I had them to tea and sherry
At the Newland Park. They said it was thoughtful.
I thought it was ironic – one last time –
A mad reprisal for their loyalty.

NICK CAVE: A PARADOXICAL EFFECT

The son of Nick Cave, Australian song-writer and author, fell off a cliff and died in 2015, aged 15. Cave sent the following thoughts to a young woman asking how to live with grief:

The paradoxical effect of losing a loved one is that their sudden absence can become a feverish comment on *that which remains*. That which remains rises in time from the dark with a burning physicality – a luminous super-presence – as we acquaint ourselves with this new and different world. In loss things – both animate and inanimate – take on an added intensity and meaning.

This feeling... of alertness to the inner-spirit of things – this humming – comes from a hard-earned understanding of the impermanence of things and, indeed, our own impermanence. This lesson ultimately animates and illuminates our lives. We become witnesses to the thrilling emergency of the present – a series of exquisite and burning moments, each extinguished as the next arises. These magical moments are the bright jewels of loss to which we cling... There is, of course, another side where we lose our resolve – we drop our guard, or just grow tired and descend into that other, darker, less-lovely world, as we disconnect and retreat deep into ourselves... These revolving feelings of connection and disconnection... are the opposing forces of loss that define our lived experience... Many of us inhabit this uncanny realm of loss – and *all* of us will find our way there in time.

Death is not an event in life. Death is not lived through... we do not live to experience death. If we take eternity to mean not infinite temporal duration but timelessness, then eternal life belongs to those who live in the present. Our life has no end in the way in which our visual field has no limits. The temporal immortality of the human soul, that is, its eternal survival after death, is not only in no way guaranteed, but this assumption will not do for us what we have always tried to make it do. Is the riddle solved by the fact that I survive forever? Is the eternal life not as enigmatic as our present one?

WORDSWORTH: THAT THOUGHT'S RETURN

This 1815 sonnet relates an episode in Wordsworth's struggle to cope with the earlier death of his daughter Catherine, aged three. Grief interrupts his present soliloquy and revivifies his intense sense of loss.

Surprised by joy—impatient as the Wind
I turned to share the transport—Oh! with whom
But Thee, long buried in the silent Tomb,
That spot which no vicissitude can find?
Love, faithful love, recalled thee to my mind—
But how could I forget thee?—Through what
  power,
Even for the least division of an hour,
Have I been so beguiled as to be blind
To my most grievous loss!—That thought's return
Was the worst pang that sorrow ever bore,
Save one, one only, when I stood forlorn,
Knowing my heart's best treasure was no more;
That neither present time, nor years unborn
Could to my sight that heavenly face restore.

We are said to be the only species that knows it must die. Why is it then distressing to learn that dolphins have been observed refusing to eat after the death of a mate? Or that geese have reacted to such a death by flying, calling and searching until disoriented and lost? Human beings can lose their appetites too, while searching metaphorically for their dead. And so it turns out that we have no monopoly on grief. Sea-lions, we learn from Didion's *The Year of Magical Thinking*, may wail when a predator kills a pup; while one Orca mother is recorded as unwilling to drop her dead and decomposing calf for seventeen days of mourning.

This book chronicles the sudden death at 71 of Joan Didion's husband, John Gregory Dunne, who suffered a fatal heart attack over dinner one evening. They met when she was writing for *Vogue* and he a staff writer on *Time*: like her he was a critically acclaimed and sometimes bestselling novelist, screenwriter and journalist. They worked from home, travelled together on joint assignments including screenplays, and collaborated on a column for the *Saturday Evening Post* which ran for years. Hollywood insiders who attended every cocktail party, they divided their time between LA and New York. In all they spent 40 years in each other's company, 24 hours a day. During every such period they confided in each other 'countless times' and shared trivial news. They fought as couples do and were happy together. Dunne read and proactively edited all her drafts from 1963 to 2003; without him she made mistakes.

The brilliant title *The Year of Magical Thinking* refers to Didion's unwillingness to relinquish her dead husband's shoes, in case he comes back and requires them. His organs had been removed and yet – like the Orca mother – she still clings to some fabulous hope. Her elegy, episodic, speculative and wide-ranging, won the National Book Award and no fewer than three glowing reviews in succession from the *New York Times*, while David Hare soon adapted it into a successful Broadway play with Vanessa Redgrave playing the lead.

This rapturous reception was qualified by Rachel Cusk who noted Didion's narcissism: why tell us, for example, that she 'wore a short white silk dress I had bought at Ransohoff's in San Francisco on the day John Kennedy was killed'? Or that one morning she and Dunne drove down from world-famous film-maker Tony Richardson's house in the hills above St Tropez where they bought fish and had coffee in the street? Or of her being invited by the pre-eminent editor Bob Silvers, after John died, to cover Democratic and GOP summer conventions for the *New York Review of Books*? Cusk finds in such references to social privilege and fame a glamorising of experience, the sin of self-importance, alienating to the 'ordinary reader'.

This misses the point. Didion knows that the people she moves among, both in LA and in NYC, share a belief in what she calls their life-management skills. They own enviable address books. They take pride in knowing the 'right people', defining themselves as such. If her mother should ever fall ill in Tunis – to pick one example she chooses – she would arrange for the American Consul to bring her English-language newspapers before putting her on a flight to Paris to be looked after by Didion's brother. This sense of entitlement is accompanied by a fear that her life will inevitably encompass events beyond even her ability to 'manage', showing human narcissism less as some specialised tragic flaw, and more as an aspect of everyday mental health. It isn't only vanity that invokes nemesis: everyone is subject to major loss. Didion has led – professionally and personally – an interesting and successful life; her account of its sudden destruction is moving and compelling.

She also has an interesting mind. She knows a lot. The reader feels directly addressed, personally and intimately. 'Marriage is memory, marriage is time,' she writes, with nifty eloquence. Such a gift or knack is not to be despised. And part of the fascination of her book is to see how little her mind helps her now. 'Until now I had been able only to grieve, not mourn. Grief was passive. Grief happened. Mourning, the act of dealing with grief, required attention.' In other words : grief is what you suffer or undergo; mourning what you find you can do about it. The whole of *The Year of Magical Thinking* is an attempt to transmute grief into mourning, while discovering no solution or panacea. We witness her struggling to understand the life that she herself lost, as well as the individual being that she lost.

What she offers amounts to a series of meditations moving fast around open questions. Within only a few pages she ponders whether she showed Dunne sufficient appreciation; wonders whether he 'knew' how he would die. 'Did he, does anyone?' Whether he experienced terror? And what, if the dead could truly come back, would they come back knowing? 'What would I give to say one small thing to John that made him happy???' She is interested in the topics of luck and self-pity. She notes how exposed, raw, fragile and unstable the bereaved appear and laments that she can no longer trust herself to present a coherent face to the world.

Towards the end of her book she presses another distinction between grief as we imagine that it might be – a forward-looking and ultimately healing, albeit painful, journey; and grief as 'unending absence' as 'the relentless succession of moments during which we will confront the experience of meaninglessness itself'. In effect, nihilism. So she battles with Macbeth's final nightmare vision of life and tries not to agree that it is a tale told by an idiot, full of sound and fury, signifying nothing.

'I realise as I write this that I do not want to finish this account,' Didion writes in her final pages. Perhaps never to finish is another symptom of magical thinking, one compounded when, in 2011, she published her sequel *Blue Nights*, elegising her adopted daughter Quintana, who died two years after her father, of flu that turned into pneumonia followed by septic shock, an induced coma, a brain bleed, five surgeries and months in intensive care.

Christina Rossetti (1830–94) has left us two of the most beautiful and popular elegies in the language. Each forecasts the grief attending the poet's future death and discusses how this might be modulated. Both, in a sense, entail looking into her future tomb, contemplating its 'darkness and corruption' and its other secrets.

Song

When I am dead, my dearest,
Sing no sad songs for me;
Plant thou no roses at my head,
Nor shady cypress tree:
Be the green grass above me
With showers and dewdrops wet;
And if thou wilt, remember,
And if thou wilt, forget.

I shall not see the shadows,
I shall not feel the rain;
I shall not hear the nightingale
Sing on, as if in pain:
And dreaming through the twilight
That doth not rise nor set,

Haply I may remember,
And haply may forget.

Opening the family tomb was a Rossetti speciality.
Christina's sister-in-law Lizzie Siddal died on the 11 February 1862 from a laudanum overdose. When she was buried
six days later at Highgate Cemetery in the Rossetti family
grave, her husband, poet and artist Dante Gabriel Rossetti consigned a manuscript of his poems to her coffin as a
grand romantic gesture. Seven years later he wanted it back.
The notebook was retrieved during a late-night Gothic disinterment which Rossetti was reluctant to attend or inform
his mother about. On 5 October 1869, two workmen removed the grave slab and prised off the coffin lid, lifted out
the desired poetry manuscript and were given beer money
for their macabre efforts before disappearing into the night.
Soon Rossetti wrote about how the notebook was 'in a disappointing but not hopeless state', further lamenting how
the poem 'Jenny' which he had 'most wanted' had a 'great
worm-hole right through every page'.

How much piety and deference are owed to the dead?
How much care and remembrance? These questions are
complicated when the poet – still young – is envisaging her
own end.

Remember

Remember me when I am gone away,
Gone far away into the silent land;
When you can no more hold me by the hand,
Nor I half turn to go yet turning stay.

Remember me when no more day by day
You tell me of our future that you plann'd:
Only remember me; you understand
It will be late to counsel then or pray.
Yet if you should forget me for a while
And afterwards remember, do not grieve:
For if the darkness and corruption leave
A vestige of the thoughts that once I had,
Better by far you should forget and smile
Than that you should remember and be sad.

'Remember' is a marvellous Petrarchan sonnet in iambic pentameters. As if the narrator fears that her beloved will not heed her request, Rossetti repeats the word 'remember' five times. Yet she also advises those mourning to feel no guilt when the claims and clatter of life supervene, releasing the bereaved from the responsibility of enshrining her in memory if this will cause pain.

Rossetti's two brilliant and moving elegies were written when she was 18 and 19, and already known – according to her first and reverent biographer, Mackenzie Bell – for adolescent *Angst*. He quotes a doctor who thought that at age 16–18 Rossetti was almost out of her mind, 'suffering a form of insanity… a kind of religious mania'. She was indeed a devout Anglican, of High Church persuasion. Vivacious and – according to her own report – short-tempered, she was advised by her doctors to over-winter by the sea. Maybe poetry also helped her achieve a balance not easily accessible in life? She wrote so many melancholy verses that her brothers facetiously referred to them as 'Christina's groans'; and she was known in later life for her piety, grimness and rectitude as also for her chronic invalidism and devotional verse such as 'In the Deep Mid-winter'.

But what is striking about Rossetti's 'Song' is that its melancholy – unlike the nightingale in the Greek legend to which it refers – is free from tragic self-pity or sorrow. And thus we see in both these poems the two qualities that Philip Larkin so admired, finding her 'unequalled for... objective expression of happiness denied and a certain unfamiliar steely stoicism'.

GRIEF AS BACKGROUND MUSIC: A.E. HOUSMAN

Although he can on occasion be witty, and even funny, the poems in A.E. Housman's *A Shropshire Lad* insist that the grief of human life is a constant. He is surely the quintessential poet of English elegy, forever bringing 'the eternal note of sadness in' as one predecessor phrased this. He is the greatest of minor poets, adept at this single note. For example, poem 31, 'On Wenlock Edge', celebrates the continuing pain of mortal existence over two thousand years, from the time of the Romans on.

> On Wenlock Edge the wood's in trouble;
>   His forest fleece the Wrekin heaves;
> The gale, it plies the saplings double,
>   And thick on Severn snow the leaves.

> 'Twould blow like this through holt and hanger
>   When Uricon the city stood:
> 'Tis the old wind in the old anger,
>   But then it threshed another wood.

> Then, 'twas before my time, the Roman
>   At yonder heaving hill would stare:
> The blood that warms an English yeoman,
>   The thoughts that hurt him, they were there.

There, like the wind through woods in riot,
  Through him the gale of life blew high;
The tree of man was never quiet:
  Then 'twas the Roman, now 'tis I.

The gale, it plies the saplings double,
  It blows so hard, 'twill soon be gone:
To-day the Roman and his trouble
  Are ashes under Uricon.

The life of the Roman is given to 'trouble', that quintessential Housman word. It recurs in other poems. Indeed, the distinguished Housman critic Peter Parker has shown how Housman, who was gay, sometimes uses this word 'trouble' as a secret way of referring to homosexuality.*

On 6 August 1895 – during the year of the two Oscar Wilde trials – Henry Clarkson Maclean, a nineteen-year-old soldier from an army family, shot himself in the Charing Cross Hotel, leaving behind a suicide note that hints strongly at his motivation: he was, almost certainly, gay and killed himself in order to avoid disgrace. Housman tucked into his copy of his published poems the newspaper account of the inquest in the *Standard*. His *Shropshire Lad* duly elegises Maclean, referring to his sexual temperament as an 'ill' that is not for mending and so cannot be cured. Its opening stanzas run:

Shot? so quick, so clean an ending?
  Oh that was right, lad, that was brave:

---

* *Housman Country: into the Heart of England* (2016) passim.

On Grief

Yours was not an ill for mending,
'Twas best to take it to the grave.

Oh you had forethought, you could reason,
And saw your road and where it led,
And early wise and brave in season
Put the pistol to your head.

Oh soon, and better so than later
After long disgrace and scorn,
You shot dead the household traitor,
The soul that should not have been born...

American poet and essayist Meghan O'Rourke in *The Long Goodbye*, commemorates her mother's life and death. She reflects:

> When we are learning the world, we know things we cannot say how we know. When we are relearning the world in the aftermath of a loss, we feel things we had almost forgotten, old things, beneath the seat of reason [...] Nothing prepared me for the loss of my mother. Even knowing that she would die did not prepare me. A mother, after all, is your entry into the world. She is the shell in which you divide and become a life. Waking up in a world without her is like waking up in a world without sky: unimaginable. [...] When we talk about love, we go back to the start, to pinpoint the moment of free fall. But this story is the story of an ending, of death, and it has no beginning. A mother is beyond any notion of a beginning. That's what makes her a mother: you cannot start the story... So much of dealing with a disease is waiting. Waiting for appointments, for tests, for 'procedures'. And waiting, more broadly, for it – for the thing itself, for the other shoe to drop... I heard a lot about the idea of dying 'with dignity' while my mother was

sick. It was only near her very end that I gave much thought to what this idea meant. I didn't actually feel it was undignified for my mother's body to fail – that was the human condition. Having to help my mother on and off the toilet was difficult, but it was natural. The real indignity, it seemed, was dying where no one cared for you the way your family did, dying where it was hard for your whole family to be with you and where excessive measures might be taken to keep you alive past a moment that called for letting go. I didn't want that for my mother. I wanted her to be able to go home. I didn't want to pretend she wasn't going to die.

MARY ELIZABETH FRYE: 'DO NOT STAND AT MY GRAVE AND WEEP'

Mary Elizabeth Clark Frye (1905–2004) was born in Dayton, Ohio, and orphaned at the age of three. A housewife and florist who lived in Baltimore, Maryland, after marrying, she wrote this poem on learning that a friend's mother had died. Because Mary was not a recognised poet, and because this poem was never officially published or copyrighted, there has been much debate over its origins and others have tried to claim it as their own or have written variations on the original.

> Do not stand at my grave and weep
> I am not there. I do not sleep.
> I am a thousand winds that blow.
> I am the diamond glints on snow.
> I am the sunlight on ripened grain.
> I am the gentle autumn rain.
> When you awaken in the morning's hush
> I am the swift uplifting rush
> Of quiet birds in circled flight.
> I am the soft stars that shine at night.
> Do not stand at my grave and cry;
> I am not there. I did not die.

JAMES FENTON: 'WHAT WOULD THE DEAD WANT FROM US?'

This poem is much read at funerals. It skilfully addresses the dark and primitive fears that underlie and infect the act of mourning. If the dead are potentially jealous of, angry and vengeful towards the living then they are in fact undead, with whom we can never be finished. They visit us perpetually; our conversations with them go on until we too are no more. Fenton has noticed that the guilt and solicitude that mourners experience – the pained concern we suffer on behalf of those who have died – has an aspect of propitiation. Moreover, since we cannot save them from their fate, memorialising can hide aggression.

So the argument flips. We're enjoined to feel the dead are secretly mourning for what they have lost. Truly to make our peace with them turns out to mean invoking their pity for us, their readiness to forgive us for having survived, and their willingness to find ways to share the stage with us.

For Andrew Wood

What would the dead want from us
Watching from their cave?
Would they have us forever howling?
Would they have us rave

Or disfigure ourselves, or be strangled
Like some ancient emperor's slave?

None of my dead friends were emperors
With such exorbitant tastes
And none of them were so vengeful
As to have all their friends waste
Waste quiet away in sorrow
Disfigured and defaced.

I think the dead would want us
To weep for what they have lost.
I think that our luck in continuing
Is what would affect them most.
But time would find them generous
And less self-engrossed.

And time would find them generous
As they used to be
And what else would they want from us
But an honoured place in our memory,
A favourite room, a hallowed chair,
Privilege and celebrity?

And so the dead might cease to grieve
And we might make amends
And there might be a pact between
Dead friends and living friends.
What our dead friends would want from us
Would be such living friends.

Eternity's a terrible thought. I mean, where's it going to end?

Every extraordinary man has a certain mission which he is called upon to accomplish. If he has fulfilled it, he is no longer needed upon earth in the same form, and Providence uses him for something else. But as everything here below happens in a natural way, the demons keep tripping him up till he falls at last. Thus it was with Napoleon and many others. Mozart died in his six-and-thirtieth year. Raphael at the same age. Byron only a little older. But all these had perfectly fulfilled their missions, and it was time for them to depart, that other people might still have something to do in a world made to last a long while.

This poem is from Gunn's marvellous and very moving evocation of courage and compassion among the first casualties of HIV, *The Man with Night Sweats*.

Memory Unsettled

Your pain still hangs in air,
Sharp motes of it suspended;
The voice of your despair –
That also is not ended:

When near your death a friend
Asked you what he could do,
'Remember me,' you said.
We will remember you.

Once when you went to see
Another with a fever
In a like hospital bed,
With terrible hothouse cough
And terrible hothouse shiver
That soaked him and then dried him,
And you perceived that he
Had to be comforted,

Peter J. Conradi

You climbed in there beside him
And hugged him plain in view,
Though you were sick enough,
And had your own fears too.

As a child Thomas Hardy was horrified by the sight of cut tree limbs and by discovering a dead bird; as an adult, death and loss figure among his most important poetic topics. He set many poems in graveyards, wrote elegies for family and friends, and other poems about memories of the dead. Although he described Queen Victoria to Lytton Strachey as a 'most uninteresting woman', on her death he wrote a 'Reverie' commemorating her.* He wrote another elegy for the death of God, imaged as a 'man-projected figure' ('God's Funeral', 1908–10).

His elegies for the dead of different wars include the unknown soldier Drummer Hodge discarded 'uncoffined' under an alien South African sky. When the *Titanic* sank, his 'The Convergence of the Twain' pictured its wreck as predestined and so unavoidable. He hymned animals such as his ill-trained dog Wessex, allowed onto the dining-table to dispute access to food with Hardy's guests; Wessex gained two elegies.

As one critic has remarked, his writing is a resurrection and safeguarding of the dead, a sustained encounter not only with the past, but with what it is like to be someone who remembers, who carries the burden of the dead.

---

* 'V.R. 1819–1901, a Reverie'. .

Certainly, his elegies are modern in offering little consolation and in their careful avoidance of false hope. Traditional elegy settles grief by inventing images of continuing energy. Hardy's by contrast view their subject-matter from a great height, the poet comforted chiefly by his own doom-struck pessimism. He coined a new word for this in his poem sequence 'In Tenebris', where the poet 'waits in unhope'. He wrote this around 1896 when his novel *Jude the Obscure* was repudiated and his first marriage wretchedly foundering. 'Unhope', as Hardy terms it, is his refuge: the poem boasts about being ultimately stripped of all illusion. In this alone he has faith.

Hardy's poetry, as has been said, is an art of losing. The Latin epigraph to 'In Tenebris', taken from Psalm 102, means 'My heart is smitten, and withered like grass.'* That Psalm is the prayer of an afflicted vulnerable person pouring out a lamentation before the Lord.

> Wintertime nighs;
> But my bereavement-pain
> It cannot bring again:
> Twice no one dies.
>
> Flower-petals flee;
> But, since it once hath been,
> No more that severing scene
> Can harrow me.
> Birds faint in dread:
> I shall not lose old strength

---

* *'Percussus sum sicut foenum, et aruit cor meum.'*

In the lone frost's black length:
Strength long since fled!

Leaves freeze to dun;
But friends can not turn cold
This season as of old
For him with none.

Tempests may scath;
But love can not make smart
Again this year his heart
Who no heart hath.

Black is night's cope;
But death will not appal
One who, past doubtings all,
Waits in unhope.

His wonderful elegy for the nineteenth century, 'The Darkling Thrush', was first printed in December 1900 in *The Graphic*, where it was called 'The Century's End'. It creates a perfect balance between Hardy's 'unhope' and his nostalgia for the pieties within which he was brought up. Keats's nightingale or Shelley's skylark had offered an alternative source of power and joy by which our world might be inspired and renewed. Hardy's thrush by contrast is elderly, and probably confused. The bleak and despairing scene he energises is scrupulously set: the light of a cold winter afternoon, the year, the vegetation, all are dying while the poor, ecstatic bird sings. Something is over, all is changing, civilisation in decay, and Hardy has no idea what will replace it. He cannot positively replace the dying with the new. The thrush is 'darkling' – unusual word – because it sings against a background of darkness, but perhaps also because the deep meaning of its song is unsure.

The Darkling Thrush

I leant upon a coppice gate
    When Frost was spectre-grey,
And Winter's dregs made desolate
    The weakening eye of day.
The tangled bine-stems scored the sky
    Like strings of broken lyres,
And all mankind that haunted nigh
    Had sought their household fires.

The land's sharp features seemed to be
    The Century's corpse outleant,
His crypt the cloudy canopy,
    The wind his death-lament.
The ancient pulse of germ and birth
    Was shrunken hard and dry,
And every spirit upon earth
    Seemed fervourless as I.

At once a voice arose among
    The bleak twigs overhead
In a full-hearted evensong
    Of joy illimited;
An aged thrush, frail, gaunt, and small,
    In blast-beruffled plume,

Had chosen thus to fling his soul
   Upon the growing gloom.

So little cause for carolings
   Of such ecstatic sound
Was written on terrestrial things
   Afar or nigh around,
That I could think there trembled through
   His happy good-night air
Some blessed Hope, whereof he knew
   And I was unaware.

The death of his first wife, Emma, in 1912 inspired his elegiac sequence the 'Poems of 1912–13' as also many later poems. By the end, his marriage had so deteriorated that Emma once idly compared Hardy to Dr Crippen, joking that he might murder her. The poems supplant the guilt-ridden and sometimes angry present with an idealised past. He also wrote a deservedly famous, wonderful elegy for himself, 'Afterwards'.* Here he paints his own tranquil and hesitant portrait as a quiet countryman who loves nature and the outdoors; he honours the separate and inward life of hedgehog and hawk, glories in the constellations of the winter sky and notices the details of country life, for example the way the sound of church bells may be broken by a cross-wind, thus making a pause. The word 'postern' in the first line means a back-door.

---

* Written between 1913 and 1916 and published in *Moments of Vision* (1917), his largest, rich, varied, confidently written and most personal collection.

When the Present has latched its postern behind
  my tremulous stay,
And the May month flaps its glad green leaves like
  wings,
Delicate-filmed as new-spun silk, will the
  neighbours say,
'He was a man who used to notice such things'?

If it be in the dusk when, like an eyelid's soundless
  blink,
The dewfall-hawk comes crossing the shades to
  alight
Upon the wind-warped upland thorn, a gazer may
  think,
'To him this must have been a familiar sight.'

If I pass during some nocturnal blackness, mothy
  and warm,
When the hedgehog travels furtively over the lawn,
One may say, 'He strove that such innocent
  creatures should come to no harm,
But he could do little for them; and now he is
  gone.'

If, when hearing that I have been stilled at last,
  they stand at the door,
Watching the full-starred heavens that winter sees
Will this thought rise on those who will meet my
  face no more,
'He was one who had an eye for such mysteries'?

On Grief

And will any say when my bell of quittance is
  heard in the gloom
And a crossing breeze cuts a pause in its outrollings,
Till they rise again, as they were a new bell's boom,
'He hears it not now, but used to notice such things'?

142

For to him that is joined to all the living there is hope: for a living dog is better than a dead lion.

For the living know that they shall die: but the dead know not any thing, neither have they any more a reward; for the memory of them is forgotten. Also their love, and their hatred, and their envy, is now perished; neither have they any more a portion for ever in any thing that is done under the sun.

VIRGINIA WOOLF: FINAL LETTER TO HER HUSBAND, LEONARD, 18 MARCH 1941

Dearest,

I feel certain I am going mad again. I feel we can't go through another of those terrible times. And I shan't recover this time. I begin to hear voices, and I can't concentrate. So I am doing what seems the best thing to do. You have given me the greatest possible happiness. You have been in every way all that anyone could be. I don't think two people could have been happier till this terrible disease came. I can't fight any longer. I know that I am spoiling your life, that without me you could work. And you will I know. You see I can't even write this properly. I can't read. What I want to say is I owe all the happiness of my life to you. You have been entirely patient with me and incredibly good. I want to say that – everybody knows it. If anybody could have saved me it would have been you. Everything has gone from me but the certainty of your goodness. I can't go on spoiling your life any longer.

I don't think two people could have been happier than we have been.

V.

FROM *ADONAIS*, SHELLEY'S ELEGY ON THE DEATH OF JOHN KEATS

On July 6 1969 the Rolling Stones put on a free concert in Hyde Park in front of a vast audience, some of whom started to assemble the evening before, carrying lighted candles. Two nights earlier, ex-Stone Brian Jones had been found dead at the bottom of his swimming-pool, which meant that the concert had a memorial flavour. Mick Jagger accordingly read two stanzas of *Adonais*, Shelley's tribute to his fellow-poet John Keats, while an aide, memorably, released many hundred white butterflies.

XXXIX
Peace, peace! he is not dead, he doth not sleep,
He hath awaken'd from the dream of life;
'Tis we, who lost in stormy visions, keep
With phantoms an unprofitable strife,
And in mad trance, strike with our spirit's knife
Invulnerable nothings. *We* decay
Like corpses in a charnel; fear and grief
Convulse us and consume us day by day,
And cold hopes swarm like worms within our
    living clay.

XL

He has outsoar'd the shadow of our night;
Envy and calumny and hate and pain,
And that unrest which men miscall delight,
Can touch him not and torture not again;
From the contagion of the world's slow stain
He is secure, and now can never mourn
A heart grown cold, a head grown gray in vain;
Nor, when the spirit's self has ceas'd to burn,
With sparkless ashes load an unlamented urn.

XLI

He lives, he wakes—'tis Death is dead, not he;
Mourn not for Adonais. Thou young Dawn,
Turn all thy dew to splendour, for from thee
The spirit thou lamentest is not gone;
Ye caverns and ye forests, cease to moan!
Cease, ye faint flowers and fountains, and thou Air,
Which like a mourning veil thy scarf hadst thrown
O'er the abandon'd Earth, now leave it bare
Even to the joyous stars which smile on its despair!

XLII

He is made one with Nature: there is heard
His voice in all her music, from the moan
Of thunder, to the song of night's sweet bird;
He is a presence to be felt and known
In darkness and in light, from herb and stone,
Spreading itself where'er that Power may move
Which has withdrawn his being to its own;
Which wields the world with never-wearied love,

Peter J. Conradi

Sustains it from beneath, and kindles it above.

XLIII
He is a portion of the loveliness
Which once he made more lovely: he doth bear
His part, while the one Spirit's plastic stress
Sweeps through the dull dense world, compelling
    there
All new successions to the forms they wear;
Torturing th' unwilling dross that checks its flight
To its own likeness, as each mass may bear;
And bursting in its beauty and its might
From trees and beasts and men into the Heaven's
    light.

XLIV
The splendours of the firmament of time
May be eclips'd, but are extinguish'd not;
Like stars to their appointed height they climb,
And death is a low mist which cannot blot
The brightness it may veil. When lofty thought
Lifts a young heart above its mortal lair,
And love and life contend in it for what
Shall be its earthly doom, the dead live there
And move like winds of light on dark and stormy air.

Concerned friends would sometimes advise the writer C.S. Lewis, mourning his wife's death, to read a work by a certain N.W. Clerk called *A Grief Observed*. In fact this book had been written by Lewis himself and published under a nom de plume. Self-inhibition is part of his story: he was shy of acknowledging authorship and probably surprised by the recognition of his book as an instant classic. Its ability to speak to us intimately and yet impersonally is still striking. Its back-story is simple. In January 1950 Lewis began to correspond with a poet from Westchester, New York called Joy, referred to in his book as 'H'. She soon moved to England, leaving her adulterous, alcoholic first husband behind. The film *Shadowlands* (1993) movingly records how Joy (played by Debra Winger) awakens the repressed and spinsterish Lewis (Anthony Hopkins) to the brave vulnerability of mutual love. She and Lewis married on 23 April 1956 at a register office. They made an Anglican marriage the following year in the Churchill Hospital, Oxford, where Joy was seriously ill with cancer. After a happy remission she died in 1960.

Lewis's book is both a diary of mourning and an essay. She brought him to life and to feeling, so that he is now in anguish. Grief is a process whose developing and recurring moods he notes. Gradually the shape of loss emerges as complex and ever-changing. Life gains 'a permanently provisional feeling... nothing stays put'. Loss is not a stable state and so it needs not a map but an evolving history. His four chapters accordingly show him thinking and feeling out loud.

He starts by enquiring how you should relate with your own wounded heart... Your former life seems still to exist, but you cannot get back to it. You feel panic, guilt, bewilderment. You also feel as if you had had a limb amputated, or rather as if the same leg were being cut off again and again. He resents it when well-meaning third parties enquire about his loss: he also records his anger when they fail to do so. The disturbed sensations of grieving can resemble fear, or being drunk, with an invisible barrier between self and other. A state of laziness or paralysis can supervene.

He soon deplores his own initial self-preoccupation and asks how he should remember the beloved wife he has lost. Involuntary memories assail him with sudden pain. Yet his conscious thoughts about her seem to make her less, not more real. Should he centre on her occasional bitterness at her own fate? Reality, looked at steadily, is unbearable. He wonders whether it can be true that the dead see us. His mental pain is as nothing compared to her bodily suffering and he ponders the meaning of the resurrection of the body without reaching any conclusion. He is in no danger of ceasing to believe in God but how should he think about Him? He risks coming to believe 'dreadful things': God as the great Vivisector, a vile practical joker, a Cosmic Sadist. God appears unreasonable, vain, vindictive, unjust, cruel, committing 'the monkey tricks of a spiteful imbecile'. His wrestling with his Faith has proven helpful to other believers.

He walks as much as he can in order to sleep better each night. He also starts to understand why grief feels like suspense: a brilliant analogy stemming from the frustration of so many habitual impulses. Thought after thought, feeling after feeling, action after action, all had Joy as their object. Now they are all of them homeless. 'She was my daughter and my mother, my pupil and my teacher, my subject and my sovereign; and always... my trusty comrade, friend, shipmate, fellow-soldier.' A kind of awakening comes when he starts to see bereavement not as a negation of love but 'as much one of its phases as a honeymoon'. Not an interruption of the dance, but the next figure. When he stops bothering about the falsity of his memories of Joy, he finds that she 'seems to meet me everywhere' – not as some ghostly revenant, but as a simple fact. He questions these moments during which he feels better. Do they represent infidelity to her memory? He finally decides that passionate grief doesn't link us with the dead but cuts us off from them. He experiences a moment of extreme and cheerful intimacy with her, one that had not passed through the senses or emotions at all: 'The less I mourn her the nearer I seem to her.'

Lewis collapsed in his bedroom at 5:30 pm on 22 November 1963, a week before his 65th birthday; his death from kidney failure followed a few minutes later. His *A Grief Observed* is a mere 64 pages long and can be read in an hour; but it packs into these pages more truth and wisdom than many much longer tracts.

When taciturn ex-President Calvin Coolidge died, Dorothy Parker (1893–1967) quipped, 'How can they tell?' There is a contrast between the brilliant public wit for which she is remembered and the loneliness and depression marking her often unhappy private life. Her poem about bereavement 'But not Forgotten' seeks a balance between private and public.

> I think, no matter where you stray,
> That I shall go with you a way.
> Though you may wander sweeter lands,
> You will not soon forget my hands,
> Nor yet the way I held my head,
> Nor all the tremulous things I said.
> You still will see me, small and white
> And smiling, in the secret night,
> And feel my arms about you when
> The day comes fluttering back again.
> I think, no matter where you be,
> You'll hold me in your memory
> And keep my image, there without me,
> By telling later loves about me.

ALBERT EINSTEIN: FINDING PEACE AND SERENITY

Albert Einstein wrote on 30 March 1936 to the grieving Queen Elisabeth of Belgium after the sudden deaths of her husband and daughter-in-law.

Today, for the first time this year, the spring sunshine has made its appearance, and it aroused me from the dreamlike trance into which people like myself fall when immersed in scientific work... Mrs. Barjansky wrote to me how gravely living in itself causes you suffering and how numbed you are by the indescribably painful blows that have befallen you.

And yet we should not grieve for those who have gone from us in the prime of their lives after happy and fruitful years of activity, and who have been privileged to accomplish in full measure their task in life.

Something there is that can refresh and revivify older people: joy in the activities of the younger generation – a joy, to be sure, that is clouded by dark forebodings in these unsettled times. And yet, as always, the springtime sun brings forth new life, and we may rejoice because of this new life and contribute to its unfolding; and Mozart remains as beautiful and tender as he always was and always will be. There is, after all, something eternal that lies beyond reach of the hand of fate and of all human delusions. And such eternals lie closer to an older person than to a younger one oscillating between fear and hope. For us, there remains the privilege of experiencing beauty and truth in their purest form... I am privileged by fate to live here in Princeton as if on an island... Into this small university town, too, the chaotic voices of human strife barely penetrate. I am almost ashamed to be living in such peace while all the rest struggle and suffer. But after all, it is still the best to concern oneself with eternals, for from them alone flows that spirit that can restore peace and serenity to the world of humans.

The present life of man upon earth, O King, seems to me in comparison with that time which is unknown to us like the swift flight of a sparrow through the hall where you sit at supper in winter, with your captains and ministers, while the fire blazes in the midst and the hall is warmed, but the wintry storms of rain or snow are raging abroad. The sparrow, flying in at one door and immediately out at another, whilst he is within, is safe from the wintry tempest, but after a short space of fair weather, he immediately vanishes out of your sight, passing from winter to winter again. So this life of man appears for a little while, but of what is to follow or what went before we know nothing at all.

W.E. HENLEY: DEATH, 'THE RUFFIAN ON THE STAIR'

W.E. Henley (1849–1903), poet, editor and apologist for British Imperialism, started out in conditions of great poverty. The precarious living he made through hack journalism was interrupted in 1868–9 by treatment in hospital for tuberculosis of the bone, and his left leg was amputated a few inches below the knee. Thereafter he had a wooden leg and walked painfully with the aid of crutches. Robert Louis Stevenson wrote to him: 'It was the sight of your maimed strength and masterfulness that begot John Silver in *Treasure Island*… the idea of the maimed man, ruling and dreaded by the sound was entirely taken from you.' With help over two years from Joseph Lister, pioneer of antiseptic surgery, he later resisted the amputation of his right leg. Henley is often derided for his defiant declaration that he is 'the master of my fate… the captain of my soul' ('Invictus'), but this sentiment has a different ring when it is recollected how bravely he fought against a painful disease, a struggle evoked in the conversational poem that follows.

> Madam Life's a piece in bloom
> Death goes dogging everywhere:
> She's the tenant of the room,
> He's the ruffian on the stair.

You shall see her as a friend,
You shall bilk him once or twice;
But he'll trap you in the end,
And he'll stick you for her price.

With his kneebones at your chest,
And his knuckles in your throat,
You would reason – plead – protest!
Clutching at her petticoat;

But she's heard it all before,
Well she knows you've had your fun,
Gingerly she gains the door,
And your little job is done.

William Ernest Henley, plagued by chronic illness and increasing pain, died at home on 11 July 1903.

JOHN DONNE: 'A BRACELET OF BRIGHT HAIR ABOUT THE BONE'

John Donne (1572–1631), poet and – later – Anglican priest, is notable for inventing an audacious and vital speaking voice in both poetry and prose. The speakers of his Elegies are 'rakish young men-about-town, addressing mistresses in tones of amorous and adulterous complicity',* famously indifferent to social mores and conventions. His early love poem 'The Relic' celebrates a chaste love affair while making fun of the Catholic veneration of saintly relics. The fearless line 'A bracelet of bright hair about the bone' is electrifying with its repeated b's, forcing us to imagine the unimaginable.

> When my grave is broke up again
>   Some second guest to entertain,
>   (For graves have learn'd that woman head,
>   To be to more than one a bed)
>   And he that digs it, spies
> A bracelet of bright hair about the bone,
>   Will he not let'us alone,
> And think that there a loving couple lies,
> Who thought that this device might be some way

---

* See John Donne, *ODNB* entry by David Colclough.

To make their souls, at the last busy day,
Meet at this grave, and make a little stay?
  If this fall in a time, or land,
  Where mis-devotion doth command,
  Then he, that digs us up, will bring
  Us to the bishop, and the king,
    To make us relics; then
Thou shalt be a Mary Magdalen, and I
    A something else thereby;
All women shall adore us, and some men;
And since at such time miracles are sought,
I would have that age by this paper taught
What miracles we harmless lovers wrought.

  First, we lov'd well and faithfully,
  Yet knew not what we lov'd, nor why;
  Difference of sex no more we knew
  Than our guardian angels do;
    Coming and going, we
Perchance might kiss, but not between those meals;
    Our hands ne'er touch'd the seals
Which nature, injur'd by late law, sets free;
These miracles we did, but now alas,
All measure, and all language, I should pass,
Should I tell what a miracle she was.

Donne was ordained in January 1615, and henceforth combined preaching in parish churches with addressing audiences at court, Lincoln's Inn, and St Paul's Cathedral. One hundred and sixty of his sermons survive, famous as intricate and beautiful pieces of prose. Among the best-known, *Meditation XVII*, which furnished Hemingway with the title of his novel *For Whom the Bell Tolls*, is a powerful, eloquent argument for human interdependence.

From *Meditations, XVII...*

All mankind is of one Author, and is one volume; when one man dies, one Chapter is not torn out of the book, but translated into a better language; and every Chapter must be so translated; God employs several translators; some pieces are translated by age, some by sickness, some by war, some by justice; but God's hand is in every translation; and his hand shall bind up all our scattered leaves again, for that Library where every book shall lie open to one another...

No man is an island, entire of itself; every man is a piece of the continent, a part of the main. If a clod be washed away by the sea, Europe is the less, as well as if a promontory were, as well as if a manor of thy friend's or of thine own were; any man's death diminishes me, because I am involved in mankind, and therefore never send to know for whom the bell tolls; it tolls for thee.

Having survived a serious illness – probably typhus – in 1623, Donne fell ill again in August 1629, and spent his last months preparing for death. He bade farewell to his friends, dealt with remaining cathedral business and posed in his shroud for the monument that remains in St Paul's today. He died on 31 March 1631, and may well himself have written the Latin epitaph on his monument.

JOYCE GRENFELL: 'IF I SHOULD GO'

Actress and comic monologist Joyce Grenfell (1910–79) is remembered for her one-woman shows on stage and TV. Her closely observed monologues caricatured the wife of a university vice-chancellor, a foreign visitor at a cocktail party, a cottager, an American mother, a cockney girl-friend… She pin-pointed their idiosyncrasies with no hint of scorn or condescension. Love of life was the keynote of her character; and her ability to speak directly to her audience comes over in her farewell poem here.

> If I should go before the rest of you
> Break not a flower nor inscribe a stone,
> Nor when I'm gone speak in a Sunday voice
> But be the usual selves that I have known.
> Weep if you must,
> Parting is hell,
> But life goes on,
> So sing as well.

Kathryn Schultz is an American journalist and Pulitzer
Prize-winning *New Yorker* staff writer. In her wise, witty
and invigorating *New Yorker* article, 'When Things go Missing', she explores both the topic of her family's absent-mind-
edness and her loss of a beloved father in a hospital ICU.
Her essay starts out in a vein of light humour, slowly deep-
ening and reaching a memorable finale in the paragraphs
that follow, with their injunction to treasure and rejoice in
our good luck – as much as or more – than lamenting our
inevitable losses.

It is breathtaking, the extinguishing of consciousness.
Yet that loss, too – our own ultimate unbeing – is
dwarfed by the grander scheme. When we are experiencing it, loss often feels like an anomaly, a disruption
in the usual order of things. In fact, though, it *is* the
usual order of things. Entropy, mortality, extinction:
the entire plan of the universe consists of losing, and
life amounts to a reverse savings account in which we
are eventually robbed of everything. Our dreams and
plans and jobs and knees and backs and memories,
the childhood friend, the husband of fifty years, the
father of forever, the keys to the house, the keys to

the car, the keys to the kingdom, the kingdom itself: sooner or later, all of it drifts into the Valley of Lost Things.

There's precious little solace for this, and zero redress; we will lose everything we love in the end. But why should that matter so much? By definition, we do not live in the end: we live all along the way. The smitten lovers who marvel every day at the miracle of having met each other are right; it is *finding* that is astonishing. You meet a stranger passing through your town and know within days you will marry her. You lose your job at fifty-five and shock yourself by finding a new calling ten years later. You have a thought and find the words. You face a crisis and find your courage.

All of this is made more precious, not less, by its impermanence. No matter what goes missing, the wallet or the father, the lessons are the same. Disappearance reminds us to notice, transience to cherish, fragility to defend. Loss is a kind of external conscience, urging us to make better use of our finite days. As [Walt] Whitman knew, our brief crossing is best spent attending to all that we see: honoring what we find noble, denouncing what we cannot abide, recognizing that we are inseparably connected to all of it, including what is not yet upon us, including what is already gone. We are here to keep watch, not to keep.[*]

---

[*] Schultz is referring here to Walt Whitman's poem 'Crossing Brooklyn Ferry': *see* 'When Things go Missing: Reflections on two Seasons of Loss' Kathryn Schultz, *New Yorker*, 13 February & 20 issue, 2017.

Acknowledgements

Thirty years ago the poet and critic D.J. Enright sent me a copy of his magisterial, witty and comprehensive *The Oxford Book of Death* (1982). With its 345 pages and 13 chapters, this anthology ranges from such topics as Suicide and Last Words, through War, Children, Animals and Epitaphs. Enright's anthology is highly recommended for readers looking to deepen or explore such topics further. I owe much to his inspiration and have borrowed some entries; others are shamelessly personal. I profited from Jahan Ramazani's *The Poetry of Mourning: Modern Elegy from Hardy to Heaney* (1994), and am also grateful to Dr Harriet Harvey Wood for suggesting entries from Scott's journal, from *Beowulf* and from Martial; and to Aurea Carpenter and the staff at Short Books for other recommendations. My understanding of Scott, Tennyson and Rossetti owes much, it will be clear, to their entries in the magnificent *Oxford Dictionary of National Biography*.

Permission to quote has been sought as follows: Elizabeth Bishop, 'One Art'; *Beowulf*, translated by Seamus Heaney; Martial's *Epigram 5.34*, translated by James Michie; the estate of Alan Turing; Douglas Dunn (*Elegies*); Nick Cave; *Wittgenstein*, translated by C.K. Ogden; Meghan O'Rourke, *The Long Goodbye*; James Fenton, 'For Andrew Wood'; Thom Gunn, 'Memory Unsettled'; Dorothy Parker, 'But Not Forgotten'; Joyce Grenfell, 'If I Should Go'.

Sources

The following list comprises secondary sources and translations to which I am indebted.

Preface

https://www.thisamericanlife.org/738/good-grief

Olive Kitteridge on being bereaved

Elizabeth Strout, *Olive Kitteridge*, 2008.

https://www.theguardian.com/books/2019/oct/19/elizabeth-trout-interview-emma-brockes [sic]/https://www.nytimes.com/2008/04/20/books/review/Thomas-t.html/https://www.theguardian.com/books/2019/oct/25/olive-again-elizbeth-strout-review

Gilgamesh: the earliest story of grief

Michael Schmidt, *Gilgamesh: the Life of a Poem*, 2019

Joan Acocella, *New Yorker*, 7 Oct 2019 'How to read "Gilgamesh"'

Sir Walter Scott: statues of snow

ODNB entry on Scott by David Hewitt

Meeting misfortune: Constantine Cavafy

C.P. Cavafy: Selected Poems, translated by Edmund Keeley/Philip Sherrard (1972)

Elizabeth Bishop: 'One art'

'Casual Perfection : Why did the publication of Elizabeth Bishop's drafts cause an uproar?', Meghan O'Rourke, *The Slate*, June 13, 2006.

The Buddha and the mustard seed

https://www.accesstoinsight.org/tipitaka/kn/thig/thig.10.01.than.html

Virgil: the tears of things

https://www.jstor.org/stable/30037962?seq=2#metadata_info_tab_contents

https://sites.uci.edu/humcoreblog/2017/10/16/sunt-lacrimae-rerum-et-mentem-mortalia-tangunt/

'Death is no more': Tolstoy

'Facing Death with Tolstoy', *New Yorker*, Mary Beard, 5 Nov 2013

The Death of Ivan Ilyich/The Devil by Leo Tolstoy – review by Nicholas Lezard, *Guardian*, 28 Jul 2011

A Stoic death: Seneca

Brigid Delaney: *Guardian* 17 March 2020. 'How not to panic during the coronavirus pandemic: welcome hard times like a Stoic'.

In Our Time with Melvyn Bragg, 'Seneca', BBC Radio 4, 23 Feb 2017

A father's grief in Beowulf

Beowulf: a New Verse Translation, by Seamus Heaney, 1999

Martial: an epigram

https://agapeta.art/2019/12/25/martials-epigrams-on-erotion/

The Epigrams of Martial, translated by James Michie (1972)

Going beyond grief: Michel de Montaigne

Michel de Montaigne: The Essays, a Selection, translated by M.A.Screech (1993)

Jane Kramer 'Me, myself and I: What made Michel de Montaigne the first modern man', *New Yorker*, 31 August 2009

Sarah Bakewell, *How to Live: a Life of Montaigne* (2010)

In Our Time with Melvyn Bragg, 'Montaigne', BBC Radio 4, 25 April 2013

The Horses of Achilles

Homer, the Iliad, translated by Samuel Butler (1898)

Rilke's dark interval

The Dark Interval: Letters for the Grieving Heart (2018), translated and edited by Ulrich Bauer

Review by Kate Kellaway, *Guardian*, 23rd Sept 2018

Tennyson: In memoriam

ODNB entry on Tennyson, by Christopher Ricks

Domesticating grief: Emily Dickinson

https://www.emilydickinsonmuseum.org/emily-dickinson/
biography/special-topics/emily-dickinson-and-death/ https:
//www.cliffsnotes.com/literature/e/emily-dickinsons-
poems/the-poems/death-immortality-and-religion

https://www.ijhssnet.com/journals/Vol_7_No_4_April
_2017/15.pdf

Wittgenstein: *Tractatus logico-philosophicus*

Translation by C.K. Ogden (1922)

The Open Tomb: Christina Rossetti

ODNB entry on Rossetti by Lindsay Duguid
https://interestingliterature.com/2016/09/a-short-analysis-of-
christina-rossettis-when-i-am-dead-my-dearest/
https://www.jstor.org/stable/26409955?seq=22#metadata_info_
tab_contents

Grief as background music: A.E. Housman

Peter Parker, *Housman Country: Into the Heart of England*
(2016)

Joan Didion: The sadness of dolphins

Blue Nights by Joan Didion, reviewed by Rachel Cusk,
Guardian 11 Nov 2011

Thomas Hardy: Waiting in unhope

Jahan Ramazani, *The Poetry of Mourning: Modern Elegy from
Hardy to Heaney* (1994)
Thomas Hardy, the Time-Torn Man, Claire Tomalin (2006);
http://personal.rhul.ac.uk/uhle/012/hardy%20introduction.pdf;
https://poemanalysis.com/thomas-hardy/in-tenebris-i/

C.S. Lewis: *A Grief Observed*

https://www.theguardian.com/books/2014/dec/27/hilary-mantel-rereading-cs-lewis-a-grief-observed

John Donne: A bracelet of bright hair about the bone

Carol Rumens, 'John Donne's song for a young couple, The Relic, skips between love, death and miracles,' *Guardian*, 10 March 2008

https://www.theguardian.com/books/booksblog/2008/mar/10/poemoftheweek31

ODNB entry on Donne by David Colclough